Seeing and Making in Architecture

You always aim to achieve that moment of insight that leads to ingenuity and novelty in your design, but sometimes it remains elusive. This book presents a variety of techniques for mapping and making hands-on design/build projects, and relates this work to real architecture. It helps you to learn new ways of seeing and making that will enhance your creative design process and enable you to experience moments that lead to ingenuity in design.

Each of the book's two parts, "Seeing" and "Making," is organized according to technique, which ranges from quantitative analysis and abstraction to pattern and scale, to provide you with a framework for mapping and hands-on exercises. Interviews with architects Yoshiharu Tsukamoto (Atelier Bow-Wow) and Jesse Reiser and Nanako Umemoto (Reiser + Umemoto) give you perspective on using these exercises in practice.

Taiji Miyasaka is Associate Professor of Architecture at Washington State University at Pullman.

Seeing and Making in Architecture

Design Exercises

Taiji Miyasaka

Routledge
Taylor & Francis Group

NEW YORK AND LONDON

First published 2014
by Routledge
711 Third Avenue, New York, NY 10017

Simultaneously published in the UK
by Routledge
2 Park Square, Milton Park, Abingdon, Oxon OX14 4RN

Routledge is an imprint of the Taylor & Francis Group,
an informa business

Library of Congress Cataloging in Publication Data
Miyasaka, Taiji.
Seeing and making in architecture : design exercises /
Taiji Miyasaka.
pages cm
Includes bibliographical references and index.
1. Architectural design--Problems, exercises, etc. I. Title.
NA2750.M63 2013
720.28--dc23
2013000143

ISBN: 978-0-415-62183-0 (hbk)
ISBN: 978-0-415-62184-7 (pbk)
ISBN: 978-0-203-49390-8 (ebk)

Typeset in Trade Gothic and New Century Schoolbook
by Gavin Ambrose

Acquisitions Editor: Wendy Fuller
Editorial Assistant: Laura Williamson
Production Editor: Ben Woolhead
Designer/Typesetter: Gavin Ambrose

In memory of my father

Contents

Contents

Acknowledgments

This book developed from my teaching at Washington State University and would not have been possible without the hard work of the students in my undergraduate and graduate architecture design studios. I sincerely appreciate the dedication of all of my students, but I must single out those whose work is included here: Alan Abdulakader, Shona Bose, Angela Brackett, Katie Chapman, Michael Dale, Monica DeGraffenreid, Jon Follett, Stephen Foster, Maria Guerra, Bradly Gunn, Laurissa Hale, Brandon Harris, Jennifer Hohlbein, Scott Jones, Mackenzie King, Lauren Kinker, Joshua Lafreniere, Matt Lamb, Mark Lo, Laurie Nii, Bobby Olsen, Orlando Orozco, Adam Pazan, Kim Petty, Nicole Reeves, and Caleb Summerfelt.

My thanks go to Stephen Foster for his significant contribution to the computer graphics in this book.

I am indebted to my colleagues for their constructive criticism and encouragement of this project. In particular, I must thank Deborah Ascher Barnstone for her invaluable advice. I also owe thanks to Nathaniel Coleman, Matt Cohen, and David Drake for their insightful criticism of the book. I have learned immensely from Paul Hirzel's rigorous and thoughtful manner of teaching. Many thanks also to Alessandra Como, Darrin Griechen, Skender Luarasi, Nickolus Meisel, Ayad Rahmani, and others for sharing in an extended, thought-provoking exchange of ideas.

Numerous others outside the university have contributed to this project. I am grateful to and thoroughly enjoyed the collaboration with Steven Rainville and Les Eerkes at Olson Kundig Architects in Seattle. I also owe my appreciation to Jim Dahmen and his family for their unwavering support and understanding of the graduate silo project, and Jeff Williams for sparking my interest in silos and helping me bring the graduate silo project to fruition. I appreciate Toyohiko Kobayashi's friendship and his insight into the work of Toyo Ito.

Countless thanks to Robert Hutchison for sharing his extensive knowledge and joining me in an ongoing dialogue on the concepts in this book. I am also indebted to Tom Hille for offering essential advice on writing a book and for giving me the confidence to try it. Leslie Van Duzer was instrumental in helping me to set up the foundation course where I started hands-on projects. Kent Kleinman opened my eyes to new perspectives on architecture when I was a graduate student. Takashi Tanaka and Tadanao Maeda have constantly encouraged me to pursue the foundations of architectural thought.

I am particularly thankful to Yoshiharu Tsukamoto for generously giving his time for the interview in this book and enlightening me with his deep understanding of architecture. My deepest gratitude goes to Jesse Reiser and Nanako Umemoto, not only for their contribution to the interview in this book but also for their many years of supporting and mentoring me in all of my architectural endeavors.

Special thanks to commissioning editor Wendy Fuller for her interest in my work, to Laura Williamson for her sustained support of this project, and to Ben Woolhead for expertly bringing this book through the editorial process to publication. I am also grateful to content editor Linda Lee for her incisive reading of my manuscript.

Finally I thank my mother, Hisako Miyasaka, for always believing in me, and my wife Jackie and son Tokuji for their infinite love and patience, without which this book would not have been possible.

Introduction

The moment when an architect arrives at a realization during the design process is when ingenuity in design is born. It is said that Louis Kahn fell out of bed in the middle of the night in his excitement when he got an idea for one of his projects.[1] Other architects may experience insights more subtly and slowly. And if architects work on a project as a group they share inspiration collectively.

A realization is not a concrete concept that occurs in an instant. It is a guideline along which a design develops. The reasons for a concept can typically be explained logically, but it is not always clear how or why the architect/designer arrived at the realization. A specific image of the design can accompany a realization, but it is often different from the final design. Insights usually occur more than once in the design process and accrue into a final design. Realization is not the end of the design process.

Although the ways architects choose to manifest their ideas can vary widely, there are recurring, common paths they take to arrive at moments of realization and achieve ingenuity in design. Architects draw sketches, make models, interact with others, and analyze and theorize to develop their design. Design may appear to be a linear process in which these activities lead directly to the moment of realization. This is why sometimes architects continue sketching until they reach that moment. However, a mere accumulation of activities does not result in ingenuity. Within these activities an abrupt and unexpectedly nonlinear leap is generally required to reach the realization.

Ingenuity is not necessarily a tangible – it resembles the increase in overall potential that occurs when an atom picks up outside energy, and an electron enters into an excited, higher-energy state. The architectural design process involves many complex constraints, and by managing, negotiating, pushing, rejecting, manipulating, and intentionally misreading these constraints, the potential for more exciting and better quality design increases. When design progresses into a higher-energy state, architects can push their design forward.

The techniques of Seeing and Making, the themes of this book, are effective and useful for learning about the design process, discovering ideas, and producing ingenuity in design. They are essential for effectively engaging with the design process.

"Seeing," as used in this book, means to explore beyond the obvious, to challenge existing perspectives, and to construct a deep understanding of what we perceive by examining and re-examining our frame of reference through careful observation, physical interaction, and imaginative inquiry. The techniques of Seeing reveal design potentials, in that they enable us to deal with constraints in architecture projects from various perspectives. They are also useful means of providing feedback on what is produced during the design process by encouraging the re-examination of the work with fresh eyes.

"Making" means to generate design ideas by experimenting with and transforming materials and information. While working with a material we discover its characteristics and can then apply this discovery toward producing something. After producing something we can gather feedback information by examining the product, and we can then use this feedback to produce something else, until we achieve the final design solution. Therefore, Making is a continuous loop of discovery, production, and (re-)examination that guides and propels the design process. Because Making results in something tangible that can be discussed, it is also useful for communicating design ideas to others.

The techniques of Seeing and Making are particularly important now, as a more complex and dynamic society has increased the number of constraints within and surrounding design projects. The multidimensional perception of reality requires that architects create more innovative and efficient ways of understanding the constraints of their projects and seeing the relationships between these constraints. Architects must utilize this understanding to examine and re-examine their design from various perspectives, because it is in this multifaceted analysis that the potential for ingenuity in design arises. Architects must seize these opportunities, see the potential within them, and transform them into design. Through Seeing and Making successfully innovative design is possible. These techniques of Seeing and Making need more attention and practice in architecture pedagogy.

This book documents exercises for Washington State University architecture design studios and seminars that took place between 2007 and 2011, and for seminars that were developed for the purpose of teaching Seeing and Making. In this book, the exercises are organized into two parts: "Seeing" (Part 1) and "Making" (Part 2). "Seeing" provides a framework for mapping exercises, while "Making" provides a framework for hands-on work.

Seeing

The mapping exercises in the Seeing section focus on exploring the ways in which students can see and observe. The intention of Part 1 is not limited to enhancing visual representation skills; more importantly, it explores innovative ways of Seeing. Students were asked to look at a single object – such as a round wooden silo or a hand – and to describe the character or identity of these objects and document their findings using various media, such as photography, charcoal on paper, ink, and plaster. This required the students to be creative in their way of Seeing and to broaden their scope of observation beyond the way they were used to looking at the world.

Entomologist Samuel Scudder, in his essay "How Agassiz Taught Professor Scudder" (1874), described the experience of learning to observe closely. Scudder's first assignment as a new research student in zoologist Jean Louis Agassiz's laboratory was to learn how to observe by examining a *Haemulon* fish. Professor Agassiz directed Scudder only to look at and take care of the fish specimen – he mentioned no objective other than observation. Within ten minutes Scudder felt that he had observed all he could. Unable to find the professor, he continued observing in different ways, for example by using his finger to feel how sharp the teeth were, counting the scales, and drawing the fish. When the professor returned many hours later and listened to Scudder's explanation, the professor criticized him for not having observed carefully enough and challenged him to look again for a very obvious feature of the animal that had gone unnoticed by Scudder. After further observation Scudder discovered one new fact after another, and the next day he answered the professor's challenge by noting that the fish had symmetrical sides with paired organs. After spending an entire three days studying the *Haemulon*, Scudder was able to analyze the similarities and differences among multiple specimens.[2] His training in scientific observation resembles what Seeing requires of students.

Our visual perception of the things around us always begins with unconscious and subjective preconceptions of the world. For example, different people interpret mountains distinctly: to some people mountains are sacred; in others they incite fear; for still others they are meant to be conquered. What we see is always informed by context – our culture, place, society, geography, climate. These constraints dictate how we see things.

It is important to understand what factors make us see things in certain ways in order to be able to search for different ways of Seeing and envisioning a project. Seeing from different perspectives enables students to design more creatively.

Making

The intention of Part 2, "Making," is not to practice building or designing a final object but rather to search for discoveries and inspirations in design through hands-on work. Making, as a bodily act, requires students to actively explore design while they physically manipulate materials. As students bend, cut, connect, stitch, press, wind, weave, and curve materials, certain ideas about what their final design will be might surface.

And because the process of handling materials is so dynamic, students confront shifting problems and are constantly forced to renegotiate their design.

This renegotiation is exemplified in anthropologist Gregory Bateson's narrative about a woodcutter, in his *Steps to an Ecology of Mind* (1972). The woodcutter believes that he alone controls his ax and the act of cutting the tree. But the reality is that the hardness of the tree trunk determines what muscle movements the woodcutter chooses for his ax swings, and the shape of the preceding cuts dictates the subsequent cut. An enormous number of conditions and factors participate in the action of cutting down a tree.[3]

The same can be said for Making. As suggested by the woodcutter story, Making involves "conversation" with a material. When a student folds a material, the properties of the material dictate how it can be folded. Through the hands-on exercises in "Making," students learn how to engage in the process of design and to invent with the materials at hand. Yet the student cannot completely predict or determine what the invention will be, since the aim is to elicit potentials from the material. This discovery of potentials is the moment of ingenuity in realizing a design solution.

Most of the time, students cannot fully recognize or identify the techniques being employed until after the exercises are finished. In other words, after seeing something, the nature of the object being viewed informs us how it should be seen; while making something, the materiality of the object informs us how it should be manipulated.

Seeing and Making in Architecture introduces the reader to a number of Seeing and Making exercises and documents Washington State University student work for each exercise. The exercises and student projects in each chapter illustrate a specific Seeing or Making technique. The student work is followed by a discussion that describes how the technique is relevant to current architecture and art, through examining the technique in the context of case studies of built and unbuilt architecture and art projects. The author's discussions illustrate how architects and artists create and implement the techniques to produce ingenuity in design. Interviews with architects Yoshiharu Tsukamoto of Atelier Bow-Wow and Jesse Reiser and Nanako Umemoto of Reiser + Umemoto expand on how the techniques in each part of the book are reflected in architecture practice and pedagogy.

Part 1

Seeing:
A Framework
for Mapping

Chapter 1
Mapping a Structure

Mapping is the creative act of visually representing information based on one's experiences, impressions, and discoveries. A cartographer selects certain information that he or she wants to communicate, and translates it into a universal visual language. In addition to physical, social, and cultural spaces, maps can represent nonspatial information. They can communicate static information that remains fixed, such as the structure, size, and texture of building materials, or dynamic information that changes, such as physical movement, temperature, and lighting.

Mapping starts with an inquiry that will direct the selection (prioritization) of information to map. Information is then collected through observation, interviews, or experimentation. Finally, the information is interpreted and displayed visually. Various visual media can be used for inventive mappings, including diagrams, photography, and even movies. This representation is less reproduction than inventive reconstruction of information to make new understandings possible.

To illustrate, let's map a cup on a table. "Cup" as a noun indicates the object, but it does not describe the coldness, hardness, or weight of the cup, which can only be perceived and experienced. You could focus your research on the surface texture of the cup. You could collect information that measures roughness comparatively by collecting rougher and smoother objects. This information could be visualized as a list of objects in order of roughness, with the cup inserted in the appropriate place on the roughness scale. Color is another aspect of the cup that could be mapped. The cup may be white, but how can the nature of the whiteness be described? Perhaps it could be expressed in relation to other colors or perhaps in terms of its age. Weighing the cup may show that it is 200 grams, but the number 200 does not in itself express how the weight feels. Can you devise your own way of visualizing, or mapping, the weight of the cup?

Mapping extends the line of vision and provides new insights about previously unseen or unnoticed aspects of an object. Such exploration of multiple viewpoints is essential in discovering solutions to design problems. In the words of landscape architect James Corner, "Mapping may generate new practices of creativity, practices that are expressed not in the invention of novel form but in the productive reformulation of what is already given. By showing the world in new ways, unexpected solutions and effects may emerge."[1]

Exercise: Silo

First, decide on a structure to investigate. At Washington State University, a timber silo in Colton, Washington was selected for the mapping exercise (Figures 1.1–1.3). The silo was built in the 1950s to store wheat, but its use was discontinued in the 1990s. It is 45 feet in diameter and 60 feet high. It no longer has a roof but is otherwise intact. The guidelines for mapping presented here are based on the silo but can be used for any structure.

Document the silo using conventional methods, such as model making, architectural drawings, and sketching. Then spend time exploring the silo and asking yourself what is interesting about it and why. You can study the silo based on structural systems, function, materials, or surrounding environmental conditions. In addition, you can observe the silo in order to contemplate elements that affect the atmosphere of the silo, such as sunlight, wind, color, smell, and texture. Viewing the silo at various times and from various distances can also be helpful.

Based on your findings, select an aspect of the silo to research further. After additional research and data collection, examine and experiment with various methods and media to visually represent the information in innovative ways.

Figure 1.1
Exterior of the silo, Colton, WA.
Photo: Taiji Miyasaka

Figure 1.2
Upward view from the silo floor.
Photo: Taiji Miyasaka

This mapping exercise will challenge your frame of
reference for Seeing. The level of innovation of the map
is based on how you see and how you choose to visually
represent whatis seen. In the sections that follow, quantitative
information and perception are used as focal points for seeing,
selecting, and collecting information in the mapping process.
Then figure/ground reversal and photography are presented
as possible ways of visually representing the information.
After highlighting exemplary mapping work by students
in the author's studios and seminars at Washington State
University, case studies are examined to learn how skills
acquired through mapping based on quantitative information,
perception, figure/ground reversal, and photography can be
used to address architecture and art.

Quantitative Information

Quantitative information is abstract data that is analyzed and mapped through various idioms, such as words, numbers, and images. Because information in architecture is becoming increasingly complex and dynamic, it is essential for architects to use several layers of quantitative information – clearly organized and visualized – to examine their projects. It is crucial not only to find interesting quantitative information but also to discover effective means of analyzing the information objectively and mapping it. Edward Tufte clearly expressed the importance of this approach: "Clarity and excellence in thinking is very much like clarity and excellence in the display of data."[2]

Figure 1.3
Interior of the silo.
Photo: Taiji Miyasaka

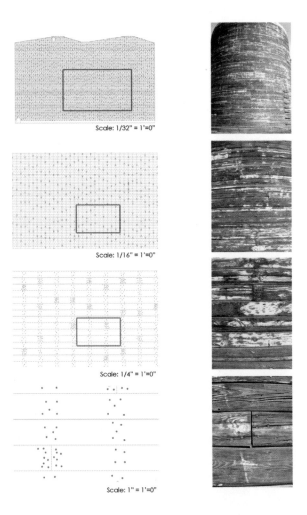

Scale: 1/32" = 1'=0"

Scale: 1/16" = 1'=0"

Scale: 1/4" = 1'=0"

Scale: 1" = 1'=0"

Figure 1.4
Mackenzie King and Kim Petty, *Nail Quantity Map*. Diagram of nail patterns in the silo. At a distance, the nails appear to follow a vertical pattern along the interior supporting structure. Zooming in reveals the unique clustering pattern.

Figure 1.5
Stephen Foster. 3D
computer rendering
showing locations
of nails.

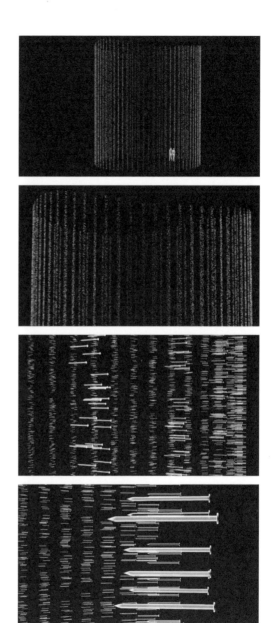

In the silo exercise, the students focused on looking for simple and clear ways to map the data. For *Nail Quantity Map* (2010), Mackenzie King and Kim Petty estimated that 130,000 nails were used in building the silo to hold together the three layers of 1-foot by 6-foot boards wrapping the 2-foot by 6-foot wood columns. The students focused on mapping the locations, types, and number of nails (Figure 1.4). The location of the nails was represented in a computer rendering that illustrates only nails, and none of the silo's other materials (Figure 1.5). The students portrayed the length and weight of the nails compared to that of other objects, such as a horse and an airplane (Figure 1.6).

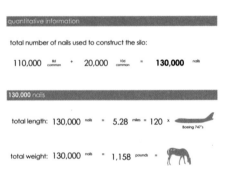

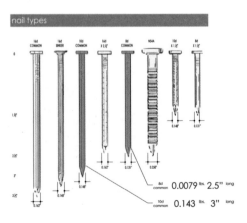

Figure 1.6 Mackenzie King and Kim Petty, *Nail Quantity Map*. Comparative diagram of nail length and weight.

Figure 1.7
Bradly Gunn, *Energy Equivalents of Pounding 130,000 Nails.*
Traces of pounding on a steel plate.

In *Energy Equivalents of Pounding 130,000 Nails* (2010),
Bradly Gunn mapped the amount of energy required to pound
the 130,000 nails. He pounded a steel plate 130,000 times so
that the deformed steel would physically show the required
energy (Figure 1.7). He also created a diagram representing
the energy using comparative data (Figure 1.8). For example,

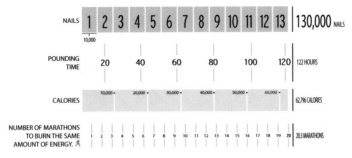

Figure 1.8
Bradly Gunn, *Energy Equivalents of Pounding 130,000 Nails.* Comparative diagram of energy used in pounding.

pounding 130,000 nails takes approximately 120 hours, consumes 62,796 calories, and is equivalent to running 20 marathons.

There are two ways of applying quantitative information in the architecture design process. First, quantitative information can be used to understand the context of a project. A common example is a topographic site map. Current mapping technology provides detailed information and allows us to understand a site in different ways – either through static maps or through dynamic maps that illustrate changes such as wind speed, solar path, and temperature. Also, maps can be used to understand the surrounding context of a site. For example, if the site is in Chicago, maps of race/ethnicity and income for the city as a whole provide additional layers of data which could help to better understand the site within a larger context (Figures 1.9 and 1.10). Quantitative analysis of the site increases awareness of the surrounding area so that the building is viewed not as independent from its environment but as part of it.

Second, quantitative analysis can be used to drive the design process. This is exemplified by the WoZoCo apartment housing project (1997) in the Netherlands, by architecture firm MVRDV (Figure 1.11). The relevance of this project to this discussion lies in the process by which the building's form was generated and the uniqueness of the building's form. MVRDV started the design process by collecting and analyzing information about physical limitations – such as the open space area, building footprint area and height, and number of units – and then generated the building design based on those quantitative constraints. For example, since they could not increase the vertical dimension because of height restrictions, the architects increased the overall volume of the building by adding thirteen units to the elevation, maximizing open space and natural light (Figure 1.12).

MVRDV produced a design solution in response to quantitative information. While quantitative information assists in understanding the context of a project, the information itself cannot generate a building's form. Rather, ingenuity in design emerges from innovatively analyzing the relationships within quantitative information.

Figure 1.9
Bill Rankin, Chicago Boundaries, Race/Ethnicity, 2009.

Figure 1.10
Bill Rankin, Chicago Boundaries, Income, 2009.

Figure 1.11
MVRDV, WoZoCo Apartments, 1997,
Amsterdam-Osdorp, The Netherlands.
Exterior photo.
© Robert Hart

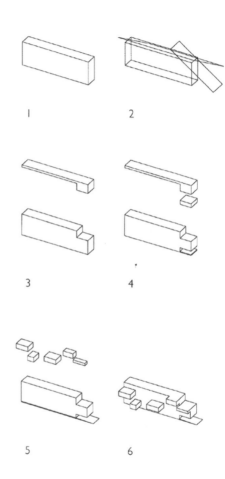

Figure 1.12
MVRDV, WoZoCo Apartments, 1997,
Amsterdam-Osdorp, The Netherlands.
Concept diagram.
© MVRDV

1

2

3

4

5

6

Perception

Maps reflect a civilization's values and sensibilities, its perception of its place during its time. The Babylonian map of 6 BC[3] illustrates the Babylonian perception of the world. The map consists of three parts: a center circle representing the ground, a circular band surrounding the center representing the ocean, and triangles representing mythical worlds attached to the circular band. Based on this map, we understand that the Babylonians perceived the world as a flat circle within a vast ocean, and believed in the existence of worlds around this ocean, though they could not experience them directly.

At first glance it may seem that this ancient people did not have a proper survey system or techniques for creating accurate maps, particularly because their mythical worlds are illustrated together with the real world. However, it is possible that the Babylonian map was created to reflect their cosmology two dimensionally, and was not intended to represent the world accurately. There could be a discrepancy between the Babylonian perception of a map's function and the contemporary one. Even though we are seeing the same, or similar, things, what we choose to perceive, prioritize, and represent is different.

When looking at the same landscape, different people perceive it differently, depending on their point of view. For example, a banker may look at a landscape from the viewpoint of profit and map the landscape on an Excel worksheet showing land value. An artist may look at the same landscape aesthetically and map the landscape in a painting. Geologist D. W. Meinig explains this discrepancy between perceptions:

> Even though we gather together and look in the same direction at the same instant, we will not – we cannot – see the same landscape. We may certainly agree that we will see many of the same elements – houses, roads, trees, hills – in terms of such denotations as number, form, dimension, and

color, but such facts take on meaning only through association; they must be fitted together according to some coherent body of ideas. Thus we confront the central problem: any landscape is composed not only of what lies before our eyes but what lies within our heads.[4]

Mapping based on perception involves examining what makes us see something in a certain way. For example, the reason that some people see a mountain as a sacred place may be rooted in collective ideas that form their history or culture. In architecture, consideration of different viewpoints can be effective in explaining why a certain building or space is considered beautiful, ugly, or intriguing.

In *Silo Perception Map* (2010), Jennifer Hohlbein and Joshua Lafreniere interviewed 29 residents near the silo and created a bar graph and model that map the interviewees' answers to the question, "What word first comes to mind when you think of the Colton silo?" (Figures 1.13 and 1.14). A pattern started to emerge in which the people who had

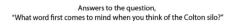

Answers to the question,
"What word first comes to mind when you think of the Colton silo?"

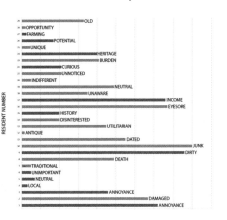

Figure 1.13
Jennifer Hohlbein and Joshua Lafreniere, *Silo Perception Map.* Bar graph.

Figure 1.14
Jennifer Hohlbein and Joshua Lafreniere, *Silo Perception Map*.
Model of the bar graph, detail.

Figure 1.15
Roni Horn, *Still Water (The River Thames, For Example)*, 1999,
fifteen offset lithographs on uncoated paper, 30½ × 41½" in
(77.45 × 105.4 cm) each, detail.
Courtesy the artist and Hauser & Wirth. © Roni Horn

lived in Colton longer tended to have a negative view, while
the newer residents either showed little interest or saw
great potential and history. Like the more recent residents,
the students expressed no negative perceptions of the silo –
they were excited about its spatial qualities, and when the
exercise was introduced to them, they discussed the value of
lumber, history, vernacular architecture, quality of materials,
and construction methods. Through mapping perceptions,
the students learned to research and examine a project from
multiple angles without making assumptions.

The ability to see from various viewpoints is essential in
professional work. Artist Roni Horn explores the nature of
perception in *Still Water (The River Thames, For Example)*
(1999), a work consisting of a series of fifteen lithographs
of the surface of the River Thames at different times, with
footnotes (Figure 1.15). By comparing images of the river,
viewers become aware of the sometimes subtle and sometimes
radical changes in the appearance of the water from moment
to moment. The same river can be seen as troubled or calm,
rough or quiet, soft or hard, pure or dirty. It can be perceived
as beautifully scenic or dark and dangerous. Horn expresses
these diverse perceptions in her lithographs and in the
following words:

The big paradox is, "How does [water] still keep its transparency?" … The water you drink, who knows how many times it's been around the world, and its appearance is still wildly constant. Obviously it's dependent on light and weather and all of these things. But water in the glass looks like water halfway around the world. It's pretty much identical.

So, there is this interesting aspect of the constancy of water and its multifarious expression … You have an identity that has an endlessly changing appearance. Or you have an identity that has an endlessly constant appearance. [Water] has both of these things.[5]

Architect Bernard Rudofsky revolutionized perceptions of vernacular architecture from around the world in an exhibition entitled *Architecture Without Architects* at MoMA in New York in 1964, and in his book *The Prodigious Builders*, published in 1977.[6] The book is based on his extensive travels in different countries and collects his photographs of vernacular architecture, from cave dwellings to tombs. According to

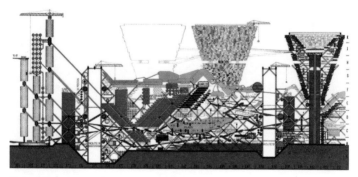

Figure 1.16
060-004-DC01 *Plug-In City*, Section, Max Pressure Area.
© Archigram 1964

Part 1 Seeing: A Framework for Mapping

Rudofsky, the lessons of buildings built by ordinary people are more significant than those of renowned works of architecture. Rudofsky's perception of vernacular architecture punctured the monolithic and dogmatic perception of modern architecture still powerful in the 1960s and became a catalyst for the postmodern movement.

Avant-garde architectural group Archigram experimented in the 1960s with plastic, in order to defy the perception of architecture as durable and immobile. The impermanence and portability of plastic inspired their designs for mobile and adaptable kinetic structures made with thin plastic. Archigram member Peter Cook captures their focus: "We have been concerned successively with the notions of throw-away buildings, of buildings which can transfer from place to place, of environments which are not made up from the complex hardware of the built form at all."[7]

Plug-In City,[8] published by Cook in 1964, was a theoretical design for a city composed of an infinitely expandable megastructure frame, movable housing elements, and public facilities (Figure 1.16). Impermanent housing is made with a thermosetting plastic shell that can be replaced easily, and other public programs are made with plastic pneumatic structures. In this project, permanence and impermanence coexist. The entire city is changeable.

The work of Horn, Rudofsky, and Archigram demonstrates that perception provides a powerful vantage point from which to generate, critique, and re-frame art and design. Individual experiences and affinities inform perception, which in turn gives insight into architecture and what it can become.

Figure and Ground

When visually representing the information selected and collected about the silo, an effective approach is to amplify what surrounds the structure instead of the structure itself – to concentrate on ground instead of figure. And when designing a building, instead of arbitrarily cutting out part of a wall to make a window, it is possible to find a suitable location, size, color, texture, and design for the window by focusing on the flow of wind or movement of sunlight, or some other external factor. Additional emphasis could be placed on other surrounding elements, for example on the neighborhood. These elements could be social, cultural, or historical. By redirecting attention from figure to ground – from structure to surrounding elements – the architect is able to create a stronger connection between building and the environment.

In *Silo-Framed Sky* (2010), Bobby Olsen and Jon Follett mapped the transformation of the sky (ground) in a sequence of photos taken through the top opening of the grain silo (Figure 1.19). The students set up a timer camera in the center of the silo floor and took photographs every 30 seconds during the day and every 40 seconds at night, for 24 hours. The total of 2,646 photographs were then stitched into a four-minute movie.

Here, rather than the silo itself, it is the sky framed by the opening of the silo that is the subject (Figure 1.17). The silo, as frame, allows the viewer to observe the subtle transformation of the sky in a more focused manner than when looking up at the limitless sky. We can see the movement of the light, clouds, stars, birds, and airplanes as if through the lens of a telescope. The appearance of the interior space in the silo also changes because of the light and shadows created over the 24-hour period (Figure 1.18). In architecture, a building (a solid mass) is typically regarded as the figure and the surrounding space as the ground. *Silo-Framed Sky* reverses this relationship.

Figure/ground thinking is evident in professional work that is situated not as independent objects in the environment but

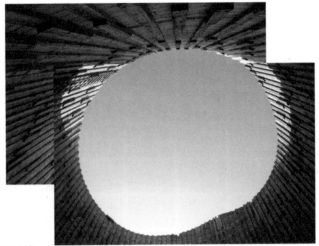

Figure 1.17
Daytime sky viewed from the silo floor.
Photo: Robert Hutchison

Figure 1.18
Night sky viewed from the silo floor.
Photo: Scott Jones

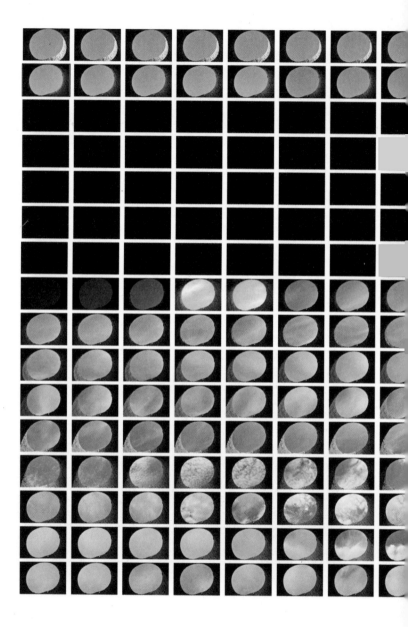

Part 1 Seeing: A Framework for Mapping

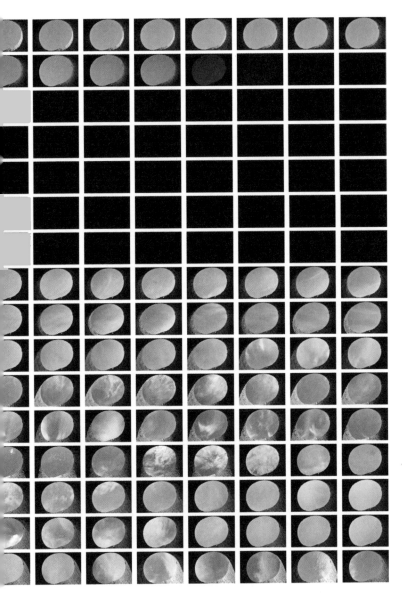

Figure 1.19
Bobby Olsen and Jon Follett, *Silo-Framed Sky*. 24-hour transformation of
the sky viewed from the silo floor.

as a natural part of the surrounding landscape. *Made in Tokyo* (2001) by Momoyo Kaijima, Junzo Kuroda, and Yoshiharu Tsukamoto is a guidebook documenting 70 non-famous buildings – *da-me* architecture, or "no-good" architecture – with a brief description, photograph, isometric drawing, and site map of each one. As the authors describe, most examples of *da-me* architecture "are anonymous buildings, not beautiful, and not accepted in architectural culture to date. In fact, they are the sort of building which has been regarded as exactly what architecture should not become."[9] In contrast, famous buildings – such as Tokyo Midtown Project (2007; Figure 1.20) and Prada Tokyo (2003; Figure 1.21) – are architect-designed, culturally or historically significant structures that, in their singularity, remain distinct from their surroundings.

Because they stand out, Tokyo's famous buildings are typically regarded as figure, while *da-me* architecture is regarded as ground. However, in reevaluating the Tokyo architectural landscape, the authors of *Made in Tokyo* viewed *da-me* architecture "in reverse," as figure. Their guidebook pays

Figure 1.20
Skidmore, Owings & Merrill, Midtown Tower
Project, Tokyo. Photo: Orlando Orozco

Figure 1.21
Prada Tokyo.
Photo: Gregory
Kessler

attention to nondescript structures such as a department store built under an expressway and housing units inserted under a railway (Figures 1.22 and 1.23). This reversal contributes to a more comprehensive view of the interdependence between architecture and the city, and helps inform design.

Figure and ground, and the inversion of the relationship between the two, can be experienced first-hand at Louis Kahn's Salk Institute in La Jolla, San Diego, California. Standing in the courtyard during the day, the mass of the building appears as figure and the sky as ground (Figure 1.24). Near sunset, figure and ground reverse: the massiveness and materiality of the building fade out, and the colored texture of the sky fills the courtyard (Figure 1.25). The sky is clearly outlined by the silhouette of the building, creating, in the words of Luis Barragan, "a facade to the sky."[10]

Although not as dramatic as the Salk Institute, the same phenomena can be experienced by walking on any narrow street between buildings. The buildings do not change in substance, but they appear completely different when the focus is displaced to the surrounding environment. By taking into consideration figure and ground when mapping the relationship between a building and its surroundings, and then switching them, students can learn to approach architecture as an extension of the environment.

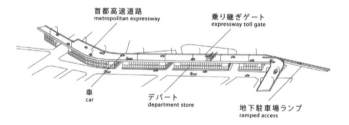

首都高速道路
metropolitan expressway

乗り継ぎゲート
expressway toll gate

車
car

デパート
department store

地下駐車場ランプ
ramped access

Figure 1.22
Atelier Bow-Wow, *Made in Tokyo*, 03 Highway Department Store.
Site: Yurakucho and Ginza, Tokyo. The department store curves along
with the expressway and extends for 500 m over two floors. The store
occupies the space where Shiodome River once flowed. The highway
is connected to lights from the underground parking facility.

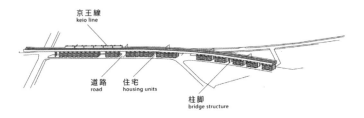

京王線
keio line

道路　住宅
road　housing units

柱脚
bridge structure

Figure 1.23
Atelier Bow-Wow, *Made in Tokyo*, 40 Centipede Housing.
Site: Hachioji, Tokyo. 43 housing units are inserted under an
elevated railway to match the structural space over a length of
approximately 300 m.

Figure 1.24
Louis Kahn, Salk Institute, San Diego.
Daytime view.
Courtesy of the Salk Institute for Biological
Studies

Figure 1.25
Louis Kahn, Salk Institute, San Diego.
Sunset view.
Courtesy of the Salk Institute for Biological
Studies

Photography

Photography is another way to visually represent information in mapping. Rather than mere documentation, photographs can become a map of an architect's worldview, ideas, and attitude toward design. They develop meanings (and interpretations) separate from the building itself, which can be analyzed from various perspectives, as Beatriz Colomina accurately expresses: "[When] built architecture enters the two-dimensional space of the printed page it returns to the realm of ideas. The function of photography is not to reflect, in a mirror image, architecture as it happens to be built … Photography and layout construct another architecture in the space of the page."[11]

In *Micro-Panorama* (2010), Caleb Summerfelt shot photographs six inches away from the surface of the silo at eye level, around the entire 140-foot long circumference. He seamlessly stitched together more than 2,000 photographs, creating a 225-foot by 18-inch collaged image (Figure 1.26). The intention was to map the texture of the silo's weathered wood through photography. The photographs bring a much higher level of detail to the wood than can be seen in reality. Subtle changes in texture, fine cracks, and white paint flecks which were actually imperceptible became visible in the photographs (Figure 1.27).

In essence, a camera does not copy exactly what we perceive, but rather opens up an unknown world. Philosopher Walter Benjamin clearly articulated the discrepancy between photographs and reality: "It is another nature which speaks to the camera rather than to the eye."[12] Because we are not able to recall memories in as clear or tangible a way as we can see photographs, it is impossible to check whether the photograph matches the memory exactly. We understand our reality by overlapping our experience (or our memory of it) with images. In this sense, images are a part of our reality.

In their short documentary film entitled *Powers of Ten* (1968), Charles and Ray Eames visualize the changing

Figure 1.26
Caleb Summerfelt, *Micro-Panorama*.
Collage of 2,000 close-up photos of the
silo's circumference.

perspectives of reality. The film begins with a one-meter-square aerial view of a man and woman picnicking in a park. The viewpoint then zooms out to a view 10 meters (10^1 meters) across. It zooms out again, to 100 meters (10^2 meters), then one kilometer (10^3 meters), and so on until it reaches 10^{24} meters, the size of the universe. The view then returns to the picnic and zooms in on the man's hand, with views 10 centimeters (10^{-1} meters) across, then 1 centimeter (10^{-2} meters), 0.1 centimeters (10^{-3} meters), and further in, until it reaches the level of quarks in a proton of a carbon atom at 10^{-16} meters. Zooming in and out changes what can and cannot be perceived about an object, creating multiple perspectives from which to see the world.

Photographs can reveal secrets about nature that have never before been seen. In the early twentieth century, German artist Karl Blossfeldt took photographs of plants magnified up to twenty times their actual size (Figure 1.28).

Figure 1.27
Caleb Summerfelt, *Micro-Panorama*. Close-up photos from the collage.

Because these photographs are monochromatic, it is easy
to focus on the forms of the plants. Blossfeldt believed that
his plant photographs exposed the logic and structure of
nature through forms. Ulrike Meyer Stump clarifies precisely
how Blossfeldt reconstructed his photographs to uncover
nature's logic: "For the publication of his plant photographs
in *Art Forms in Nature*, Blossfeldt created details of details,
scrupulously removing all traces of his working methods …
At a later stage, he sometimes retouched undesirable features,
removing them from a print."[13] Blossfeldt, whether consciously
or unconsciously, must have had a certain idea about the logic
of nature, which is why he felt a need to alter his prints to
project it.

Figure 1.28
Karl Blossfeldt, *Achillea umbellata* (Yarrow).

Architects Jacques Herzog and Pierre de Meuron visually represented Blossfeldt's photograph of a leaf on the facade of the Ricola Europe Factory and Storage Building in Mulhouse, France, built in 1993. An enlarged image of the leaf was silkscreened onto polycarbonate panels that were repeated on the facade. The image of the leaf appears blurry because of extensive repetition and enlargement of the image (Figures 1.29 and 1.30).

Herzog remarked on the intentions behind his manipulation of the leaf photograph:

> The size of the leaf was unbelievably vital to this project ... [I]f the motif were smaller, it would look like a bathroom tile and then it would be ridiculous. If it were much bigger, there would be a one to one relationship between human being and leaf, so to speak, and that doesn't work either because then people would be addressed much too directly.[14]

The original leaf photograph was transformed from paper into polycarbonate and came to be viewed as a construction material. In this way, Herzog and de Meuron often produce new ways of seeing materials through their design.

Photographer Thomas Ruff's work can be regarded as an extension of Herzog and de Meuron's architecture. In addition to the Ricola Mulhouse building itself, Ruff photographed the leaf on the polycarbonate panels of the building with a night-vision camera and touched up the photograph electronically (Figure 1.31). Art historian Catherine Hürzeler insightfully comments on how Ruff's photograph appropriates the leaf and causes it to persist beyond Herzog and de Meuron's work: "Ruff's photograph lends Blossfeldt's relief-like rendition of the leaf motif a singular aura and in its reiterated arrangement, it turns into something else again, something new."[15]

Figure 1.29
Thomas Ruff, Ricola, Mulhouse, 1994, chromogenic color print, 188 × 285 cm.
Courtesy David Zwirner, New York

Figure 1.30
Leaf motif based on a photograph by Karl Blossfeldt.
Photo: Margherita Spiluttini, Vienna

In this sense, Herzog and de Meuron's architecture did not end when their buildings were completed. The photographer's viewpoint – visible in every picture – communicates the author's perspective. Ruff says, "You don't have to trust pictures; you just have to respond to them; if you manage to communicate with them, they evoke associations and feelings, which is exactly what happens in Herzog and de Meuron's constructed reality."[16] Thinking of photographs not as copies of reality but as materials that communicate new and different ways of seeing reality can be immeasurably helpful as a creative way of envisioning information in the mapping process.

Figure 1.31
Thomas Ruff, Nacht, Blossfeldt, 1994, color photograph
8 × 8¼ in (20.3 × 21 cm), Edition of 35.
Courtesy the artist and Peter Blum Edition, New York

Chapter 2
Mapping a Physical Movement

Exercise: Hands

Contemplate how you perceive the environment through your body. How do your senses work together? When you look at a building, how do you move your head and eyes? Do you move any other part of your body? When you enter a room, do you bend your body? Which part of your body goes in first? When you climb stairs, which parts of your feet touch the tread?

This is a mapping exercise to capture hand movement. Observe how your hands take information from the environment and act in response to it. Then represent your observations with a material. Consider the choice of material(s) carefully, to present the observations in a map in the most effective way. (Video recording should not be used to document hand movements, because it does not provide a direct relationship between the hands and the materials used for mapping.) Craftsmanship during the design process is as important as it is for the solution.

We often do not think consciously about how our hands move. By observing hand movements carefully, we will see what the hands are capable of doing and how they act and respond to the environment. This will show that our bodies can act beyond our consciousness. In relation to architecture, we assume that we perceive buildings and space consciously, but our bodies may also experience buildings and space reflexively through the senses. This exercise will provide a greater understanding of how our bodies experience buildings and space and how to apply this understanding in design.

Observing Hands

Hands make a lot of our activities possible. Hands hold things, cook food, play instruments, type words, throw balls – the list is endless. Our hands design, make sketches, models, and drawings, and construct.

While writing, we do not look at our fingers or hand holding the pen. We look at the black lines from the pen. Our fingers seem to follow naturally the movement of the pen. We realize that we do not know exactly how we hold the pen with our fingers. If someone asked us to describe how we hold the pen or how we move our fingers to write, we would have to observe and think about it carefully before we would be able to explain. It would be difficult to describe even after observing the movement carefully. Although we may think we are aware of how to control our hands, they execute very complex movements without our conscious understanding. We may not know exactly what hands are capable of doing.

In *Daily Hands* (2006), Michael Dale uses liquid latex as a material for mapping the movement and interaction of his hands during daily activities such as holding a cell phone, writing, and brushing his teeth (Figure 2.1). Dale first applied the liquid latex to the hand, which interacted with commonplace objects while the latex was vulcanizing. The result is a series of three-dimensional imprints indicating how the hand touches, anticipates, moves, and accommodates the use of daily objects.

Inverted Hands by Maria Guerra (2006) focuses on the tortilla-making process and maps the relationship between tortillas and the hands that make them. Tortillas with handprints on them were cast in plaster during four stages of tortilla preparation in order to show traces of the handprints (Figure 2.2).

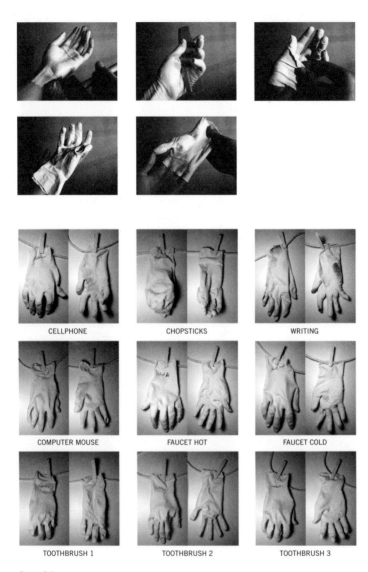

Figure 2.1
Michael Dale, *Daily Hands*.

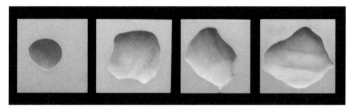

Figure 2.2
Maria Guerra, *Inverted Hands.*

Imprint by Nicole Reeves (2006) maps the hands' activity on a computer keyboard during the course of five minutes, while engaged in different tasks (Figure 2.3). Reeves placed a sheet of copper mesh on the computer keyboard and typed with black ink on her fingers. The traces of ink on the copper sheet differed depending on the activity, for example typing an email or online banking. *Imprint* shows how the design of the keyboard controls the movement of the fingers.

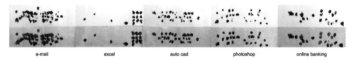

| e-mail | excel | auto cad | photoshop | online banking |

Figure 2.3
Nicole Reeves, *Imprint.*

These mapping projects show that the shape and movement pattern of the hand are strongly connected to the forms of objects. For example, if our hands were spheres with fingers projecting in all directions, keyboard design would be quite different. The keyboard would be curled up so that the fingers could reach the keys. The forms of many products and objects are developed in relation to the hands.

Human Movement in the Built Environment

The evolution of humans from walking on all fours to walking upright on two legs freed the hands and resulted in the development of tools. With the invention of tools, humans were able to harness environmental resources and information, and ultimately alter the environment.

When we interact with the environment, we use our entire body and all of our senses. Therefore it is important to learn about and connect with the environment. Architects transform environmental resources into design. Architects can discover potentials of the site where a building will be constructed by considering the relationship between the environment, the building, and the client.

As one means of connecting buildings with the environment, architects can include human figures in their drawings. This not only provides a sense of scale, but also suggests architects' understanding of how humans might respond to the building and its surrounding environment. Architect Glenn Murcutt's sketches and section drawings of Done House include human figures, envisioning how people might engage with the house. In the sketches of the courtyard from the vantage points of the roof terrace and the stairway to the roof terrace, human figures drawn in front of the courtyard windows are looking at the pool and adjacent trees (Figure 2.4). In the section drawing (Figure 2.5), human figures are drawn in almost every room. For example, in the courtyard, there are three people – two at the pool and one on a chaise longue. There are two people standing in the middle of the exterior stairs and looking down at the courtyard. Thus, the courtyard is like a theater stage, with performers and an audience. The section drawing shows four figures on the roof terrace – the highest number of people in one room – so we can infer that this is the most public place in the house. Two people are standing at the center of the terrace and two are sitting on sofas by each wall. In this section, a total 16 people are drawn. Given that this is a private residence, human figures

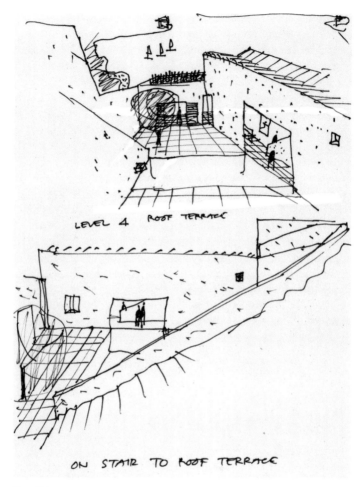

LEVEL 4   ROOF TERRACE

ON STAIR TO ROOF TERRACE

Figure 2.4
Glenn Murcutt, Done House, Mosman.
Perspective sketches. Courtesy Mitchell
Library, State Library of NSW – PXD 728/185.
© Glenn Murcutt

are drawn more to indicate how spaces in the house could be utilized than to show the actual number of occupants. By looking at the space through the human figures shown, we can understand the architect's view of how people might inhabit the building and space.

"Architecture Comes from the Making of a Room" (1971), a drawing by Louis Kahn, also reveals an architect's thoughts on how people might occupy a space (Figure 2.6). The room in Kahn's drawing contains a vaulted ceiling, fireplace, and window. In front of the window are two human figures, one drawn with a dark line (the speaker, presumably) and the other with a lighter line (the listener). The text in the drawing reads: "The Room is the place of the mind. In a small room one does not say what one would in a large room. In a room with only one other person could be generative [sic]. The vectors of each meet." The sketch and incorporated text suggest Kahn's belief that this room might be ideal for inspiring intimate and thoughtful conversations between people.

Kahn's use of human figures in his drawing shows his deep understanding of human behavior in the built environment. Such an understanding of human behavior and physical

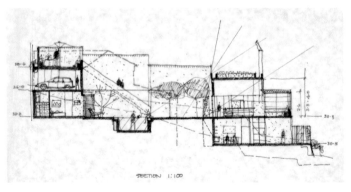

Figure 2.5
Glenn Murcutt, Done House, Mosman. Section drawing.
Courtesy Mitchell Library, State Library of NSW – PXD 728/185.
© Glenn Murcutt

Within the drawing (handwritten):

Architecture comes from The Making of a Room

The Plan A society of rooms is a place good to live work learn

A great American Poet once asked the Architect 'What slice of the sun does your building have, what light enters your Room as if to say the sun never knew how great it is until it struck the side of a building.

The Room

is The place of the mind. In a small room one does not say what one would in a large room I in a room with only one other person could be generalized The vectors of each meet. A room is not a room without natural light. natural light gives the time of day and the mood of the seasons to enter.

Figure 2.6
Accession #1972-32-4, Louis I. Kahn, "Architecture Comes from the Making of a Room," drawing for the *City/2* Exhibition, 1971, charcoal on yellow tracing paper, 33¾ × 33¾ in (85.7 × 85.7 cm).
Philadelphia Museum of Art: Gift of the artist, 1972

movement contributes to ingenuity in design, because it illuminates the constraints and potentials that architecture projects must innovatively address. Mapping a hand movement or other physical movement is an effective strategy for learning essential skills for thinking about how humans circulate in and engage with architecture.

Chapter 3
Mapping a Narrative

Exercise: Remembrance

Space is unquestionably linked to experience. When we design buildings, we design based on what we know, have seen, have heard, and remember. This mapping exercise explores the construct of memory. It focuses on discovering the potential of the narrative of memory to inform and generate design. It will enable you to engage with the design process by accessing your memories.

Think of a deceased person whom you want to remember. What do you remember about him or her? Do you have a memory of what you did with him or her? Does a specific location or moment cause you to remember him or her? Is your memory of him or her accompanied by a specific smell, sound, taste, or touch? Describe in words or in a sketch what comes to your mind when you recall him or her. Be specific about your relationship with the person.

Next, map your memory of the person visually. Select the materials carefully. The materials chosen may symbolize the relationship, or their transformation may illustrate the relationship. Present your map and a narrative text that explain the relationship.

Memory-Inspired Mapping

The idea for this mapping exercise came from the author's experience of designing an urn for his father. He approached the design by selecting objects that evoked memories of his father and transformed the mass of objects into an urn by casting them in white concrete and firing them in a kiln. The objects burned away and created a void space inside the concrete. The unseen form of the void became a map of the author's memories and holds his father's ashes.

The process of mapping a memory starts with selecting a series of vignettes from the myriad memories we have of a person. Each vignette describes a brief encounter or memory but encapsulates the relationship with the person. Then these abstract narratives of memory are contemplated from various angles and reconstructed in visual form to produce a design.

For *Creek Walk* (2010), architecture student Jennifer Hohlbein mapped her memory of her grandfather, a former marine biologist, by subtly weaving his important research papers and personal photographs into yarn, to represent a river or path where they spent time (Figures 3.1 and 3.2). Hohlbein poignantly and vividly describes the vignettes that she chose to map from her collection of memories:

> My grandfather was a difficult man to get to know, famous for being humble and reserved. As soon as you thought you knew everything about him you would quickly discover another quality that was hidden deep down. *Creek Walk* is a representation of this, showing multiple layers, weaving in and out, implying that even if you think you know everything, there are still pieces of him that are tucked away. As a child he would take me on walks down creeks and we would locate the salmon redds for his marine biology research. He would ask me to mark the upturned gravel using a stick buried into the creek bed with twine tied on top. The scent of twine on my

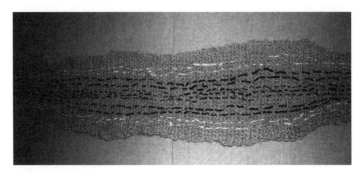

Figure 3.1
Jennifer Hohlbein, *Creek Walk*.

Figure 3.2
Jennifer Hohlbein, *Creek Walk*. Detail.

hands would linger for hours afterwards and became a scent and texture that I will forever carry with me. It was during these creek walks that I felt I got to know him the best.

Hohlbein's personal narrative informs her design. It serves as a concrete intermediary between abstract memory and abstract design. Her design expresses her personal connection with yarn, as a substitute for the twine mentioned in her narrative. Hohlbein's process of mapping a memory is successful because it forms a strong link between the selected memory, the narrative of the memory, and the visual representation of the memory.

Four Characters (2011) by Mark Lo maps his cultural connection to his Taiwanese grandmother. He selected an old Chinese text; on it he highlighted the four Chinese characters that also occur in his grandmother's name, which are among the small number of Chinese characters that Lo knows (Figure 3.3). Through the act of searching for these four characters among the thousands of unfamiliar characters, Lo remembers her. This is Lo's narrative on the project:

羅楊六妹 (Lo-Yang Liu-Mei) is my grandmother's name. She is Taiwanese and that makes me Taiwanese, although I do not retain much of this culture. Being born and raised in the United States disconnects me from my heritage. The only link I have is through my grandmother. There are thousands of characters in the Chinese language that are symbols of my heritage but remain incomprehensible to me, except for the four that I will never forget: 羅楊六妹.

Just as the narrative describes Lo's memory of his grandmother as his only link to all of Chinese culture, the highlighted characters represent the only part of the book that he recognizes. The narrative successfully informs Lo's mapping process and results in a simple yet thoughtful design.

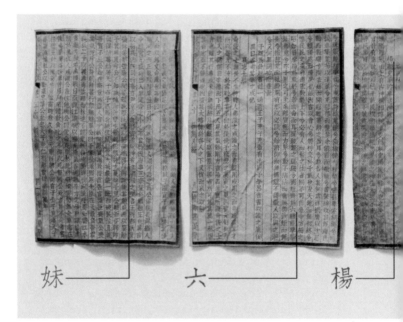

妹　　　　　六　　　　　楊

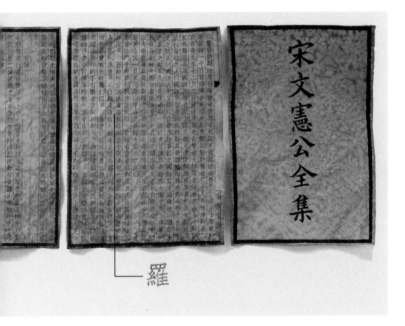

Figure 3.3
Mark Lo, *Four Characters*.

The Role of Memory in Designing the Jewish Museum Berlin

Daniel Libeskind's architecture is often inspired by memories and history. His design of the Jewish Museum Berlin (1999) reflects on the history of the Jews in Germany through its architectural spaces: ground plan, voids, underground passageways, and garden (Figure 3.4). The tortuous, zigzagging ground plan of the building resulted from the architect's plotting of the addresses of random Jews and pairing them with prominent Jewish and German citizens on a map of prewar Berlin in such a way as to form a broken Star of David (Figure 3.5). Libeskind designed a cut that passed through this zigzag form, which he regards as a void that symbolizes the erasure and emptiness of Jewish history in Berlin.[1]

Figure 3.4
Jewish Museum Berlin, aerial photo.

Figure 3.5
Conceptual drawing, star plan, Jewish Museum Berlin.
© Studio Daniel Libeskind

The building has three intersecting underground passageways that narrate the paths of the Jews in Germany: the Axis of Continuity, the Axis of Emigration, and the Axis of the Holocaust. The first and longest one, the Axis of Continuity, connects the old building to the new one and symbolizes the continuation of Jewish life in Berlin (Figure 3.6). The Axis of Emigration leads outside to the Garden of Exile (Figure 3.7). The floor of this passageway is uneven and gradually ascends, and the walls are slanted and close in gradually, until the

Figure 3.6
The Axis of Continuity leading to the Sackler Staircase.
© Jewish Museum Berlin. Photo: Jens Ziehe

passageway ends with a heavy door that opens into the garden. The tunnel represents the disorientation and difficulties experienced by Jews driven into exile, and the Garden of Exile portrays exile as the way to freedom. But this was not true freedom, as evidenced in the vegetation that was placed out of reach at the top of pillars and the tilted foundation that made people feel disoriented. The third passageway, the Axis of the Holocaust, becomes narrower and darker as it leads to a dead end at the Holocaust Tower. The Holocaust Tower is pitch black, with a sliver of light filtering in from a slit in the roof. Libeskind's design for this tower was based on his memory of the story of a Holocaust survivor, who recalled the hope that came from having been able to glimpse the sky through the slats of the boxcar in which she was riding to a concentration camp.[2,3]

Libeskind's design for the Jewish Museum Berlin is a narrative that pays homage to the history of the Jews in Germany. Libeskind confidently articulates his goal of designing a building embodied with memories: "What was needed, as I saw it, was a building that, using the language of architecture, speaking from its stones, could take us all, Jews and non-Jews alike, to the crossroads of history."[4]

The narrative process of remembering is more important than the final design product here. While other exercises have required you to map something perceived in reality, this exercise required you to map something abstract. The invisible/nonexistent/imagined is brought into reality and visualized in mapping based on the narrative of memory. In remembering, we create a narrative, which helps us to give form to memory. By reaching out to the imagination or creating a narrative we are able to bring the abstract into reality as design.

Figure 3.7
The Garden of Exile.
© Jewish Museum Berlin.
Photo: Jens Ziehe

Interview 1:
Yoshiharu Tsukamoto,
Atelier Bow-Wow, Tokyo

Atelier Bow-Wow is involved both in design and in researching buildings and cities. Their research results have been published in books such as *Made in Tokyo*,[1] *WindowScape: Window Behaviourology*,[2] and *Pet Architecture Guide Book*.[3] Atelier Bow-Wow's way of seeing cities, buildings, and building elements in these books challenges existing perspectives of architecture.

Observation

Taiji Miyasaka: Your book *Made in Tokyo*, published in 2001, is a very intriguing documentation of your observations of vernacular buildings in Tokyo. I'm interested in what you mean by "observation." How is it different from "research"?

Yoshiharu Tsukamoto: In my university research, I use typology as a method of looking at society through architecture. My research is unique in that it looks at environment and society, as a physical environment, through the lens of architecture. Atelier Bow-Wow's way of looking at the city is not based directly on population data and other statistics. Buildings don't talk, but they do narrate. It is our job to speak on their behalf, which leads to inward observation of architecture.

TM: You worked for ten years on *Made in Tokyo*, and many people were involved. Does observation change depending on who is involved and with the passage of time? For example, does observation fundamentally change somehow depending on whether it is done by an individual or by a group?

YT: No, it doesn't change much. As I said before, architecture narrates, but we put into words what it does not say in words. The fact that architecture observes means that we too can observe. As long as buildings don't change, observation shouldn't change, regardless of how many people do it.

TM: Does that mean we can understand buildings better if we try to put ourselves in their place and observe from their perspective?

YT: I wouldn't personify buildings to that extent, but, through buildings, we can understand society's way of thinking, climate, and material constraints at the time the building was built. This illuminates on society, that is, human living conditions. Buildings actually tell us the conditions under which people live. The most important thing is whether or not one can see architecture in this way. For this purpose, literacy is necessary. Kaijima and I have repeatedly gone to many places and seen many buildings, so we have developed literacy. Because of this, we have become able to understand what kind of observations are represented in buildings, what characteristics a certain place has, and what kind of society created these.

TM: How exactly does literacy help to see? Does it develop the intuition necessary for seeing?

YT: No, it's not intuition. Buildings have their own inherent structure. For example, they have roofs, walls, columns, and windows, and each of these are laid out not arbitrarily, but according to certain natural laws. They obey the laws of gravity, and when architectural elements are considered based on the intention of separating interior and exterior, they naturally are laid out in a certain way. After seeing this time after time, when there are slight differences it becomes possible to understand why these differences occur. This is similar to our way of looking at vernacular architecture. When looking at vernacular architecture, many things can be understood from differences in the layouts of building elements. In *Made in Tokyo* we were more interested in why a building was built, so we looked at the relationship between the urban environment and architecture, the combination of programs, and the thinking of the people who needed these.

TM: Given Tokyo's fast pace of tearing down old buildings and constructing new ones, it would seem that if you were to publish another *Made in Tokyo*, the content might be very different from the original book published in 2001.

YT: We may include historical factors a little more. I have a general idea of how the city of Tokyo has changed over the past 150 years, so the question would be how to place individual buildings within that historical perspective. In that sense, the buildings that we choose to observe do not have to be unique, as long as they can tell us vivid stories about history.

TM: By looking at buildings over time, we can start to understand the lives and thinking of Tokyo residents at various points in time based on the similarities and differences in the layouts of buildings.

YT: That's right. When we were working on *Made in Tokyo*, we observed buildings from the perspective of the "here and now" without thinking historically. I mean, if we wanted to, we could have learned about the history, but what would the point be of just studying the history? We focused more on what was happening in the "here and now." Most of the buildings in *Made in Tokyo* are no more than 20 to 30 years old, so they don't have a very long history but some time has indeed passed since their construction. We did not concern ourselves much with this in *Made in Tokyo*, but now we have also become interested in the rhythm of the city and the transformation of architecture over time.

TM: I think it would be very enlightening to see a new version of *Made in Tokyo*, which adds a historical component to the original *Made in Tokyo*.

Representation

TM: In *Made in Tokyo*, not only observation but also representation is important. Does "representation" refer to how we express what was observed?

YT: You seem to be asking about observation and representation from the perspective of research and the presentation of research results, but I believe that observation and representation are matters involving a building's way of being.

For buildings, which are enduring and impactful, the decision of what to observe is important, but I think it is more important to know what to represent. In other words, observation is about the "here and now," but representation is related to the past and future and the elsewhere, instead of the "here and now." Therefore, through representation, we examine what is observed with a wider timeframe and geographic area. Based on what is represented, we choose what to observe.

In designing architecture, there are many things that we think of once but end up not doing. We may think of many things that should be considered, but then realize in the overall context that they are not important, shouldn't be reflected in the building, or are matters that can be resolved by simply explaining to the client.

For example, a room becomes hot, so we install an air conditioner. Behind this is the observation that the room becomes hot under the current conditions. If the windows open, air circulation is good, and the room is cool, then there is no need for an air conditioner. In the first case, the fact that heat becomes trapped in a place without good air circulation is observed as a problem, and an air conditioner continues to represent this problem while resolving it. Meanwhile, in the second case, the heat problem is no longer a problem because the windows are equipped with an opening/ closing mechanism. In other words, this is where the difference is, in defining what is viewed as the problem. In many of the world's buildings, architects focus on minor problems and address these materially. They can't sell anything and don't earn any money unless they solve these minor problems materially, so they do so, but there are any number of ways to get through a project without doing this. What must be done when designing a building is to carefully select the most important, true problems.

This can be said not only for buildings, but also for urban planning. For example, in the 1960s and 1970s, single-family houses and apartment buildings were built in order to accommodate the population influx to cities, but now second-generation residents prefer not to live in these suburbs because they dislike the long commutes, so the working population is decreasing. This is because housing was built based on short-term thinking, and if viewed from a long-term perspective I think there probably would have been other options. If they had looked for land near the city center when deciding where to build new housing and built high-rise buildings to allow for high-density living, the next generation also could have lived there. They optimistically developed suburban areas without considering the impact that the provision of housing would have in the future. This lack of an exit strategy shows how simplistic the method of representation was. They could have chosen to not root newcomers in architecture – that is, to not address the issue of housing materially. For example, tax incentives could have been created that would have made it easy to rent spare old houses to people who came from rural areas, or there may have been other ways to absorb the excess population. Building houses in the suburbs is a policy that is advantageous to industry, from infrastructure to housing and automobiles.

TM: How do you decide what method of representation to use within the context of feedback between observation and design?

YT: Decisions can be made at various stages regarding what to represent, but the way in which a building is designed based on these decisions is design thinking. By extension, this also leads to the invention of representation methods.

TM: Atelier Bow-Wow has designed many houses, but how does one's design thinking figure into actual design?

YT: We think while we design, so perhaps design thinking does not come first. The accumulation of decisions leads to a certain design thinking in the end. Even so, a historical recognition of where we are and what we are doing at present is at work. The direction we take with respect to the historical positioning of a project is definitely part of design thinking, but unfortunately it is pointless unless we delve into the meaning of our decisions at each stage.

TM: It is important to examine every decision.

YT: Whatever we do generates problems and new aspects. For example, let's suppose we have a problem A and an answer B which solves problem A. In this case, A and B work together well. However, if B makes a problem C, then we have to reconsider B. In other words, there are many possibilities for B in response to A, but in fact B must also respond to C. This is what design is all about. It is the integration of many things.

Students usually cannot apply this feedback process. They don't understand that their ideas may create a problem, so they continue without feedback, and their ideas do not develop. When we design with feedback, everything suddenly appears resolved. This is when a design becomes finalized.

TM: Atelier Bow-Wow's feedback system seems quite complex. For example, when you were designing *Pony Garden* [2008], the place for ponies was defined first, followed by the client's living area (Figures I1.1 and I1.2). In that case, wouldn't your decisions differ depending on whether the feedback was from the perspective of the ponies or the client?

YT: I am interested in the fact that architecture not focused on humans is actually more comfortable for people. Isn't it just a certain kind of ideology that we have to make architecture for humans? It is very egocentric to ask what architecture for humans is. Fundamental discussion of why it should be for humans in the first place is missing.

Figure I1.1
Atelier Bow-Wow, *Pony Garden*.
Garden side facade.

Figure I1.2
Atelier Bow-Wow, *Pony Garden*.
Feeding pony from the house.

Pedagogy

TM: When you teach university architecture design studios, do you ever give assignments relating to observation?

YT: In studios I try to teach what authenticity in architecture is. Without knowing this, students cannot understand what the problems and difficulties are in architecture. However, when studying authentic architecture, it is not interesting to just memorize types of architecture, so I try to talk with students as much as possible about what kind of society a certain type of architecture illuminates and why this type of architecture evolved.

TM: Can you be more specific about how you teach authentic architecture?

YT: Basically, I teach typology. Even individual buildings are based on an underlying type, and by understanding this, it should be possible to comprehend violations, deviations, and variations (Figures I1.3 and I1.4). I ask students to be aware of what lineage of typology they are working in. If we list the conditions under which a certain typology develops, it appears that we are explaining the composition and type of architecture, but actually this enables us to see how humans live. In this sense, we can also reorganize our lives through architecture. There are different places from where we are now, and we start to see the possibility of different people settling there. This also means that we ourselves become different people. Seeing architecture in this way is broader and more interesting.

TM: When students study typology, do they sometimes go outside with cameras and sketchbooks and learn about typology while observing actual buildings?

YT: When I was working on *Made in Tokyo*, I asked students to look for buildings, and then we would discuss the buildings that they found. However, recently I have been trying a slightly different approach. Now I am teaching in Kyoto, and I ask students to choose

Figure I1.3
Gallen-Kallela
Museum, Espoo,
Finland.
Photo and diagrams
by Tokyo Institute
of Technology,
Graduate School
of Architecture
and Building
Engineering,
Tsukamoto
Laboratory

a spatial device that evokes the ethos of what I call Japanese "landscape-ism" from a scene in *The Old Capital,* a novel by Japanese author Yasunari Kawabata that takes place in Kyoto. Then they actually go to see what the place is like now, and on a large sheet of paper they draw the overall scene in which the spatial device is positioned. Next, using this drawing as a template, they produce a design based on how they think the scene will change and evolve in the next generation, given the current conditions. In other words, they think about architecture and urban space through the eyes of Kawabata instead of through only their own eyes, which tend to see only the "here and now."

TM: Using a novel as a starting point for observation is an effective method for having students think about space and architecture in the context of a clear timeline.

YT: One thing that it is possible to do in architecture design is to create a place for humans in response to the question of where we are and what we are doing now. This means a place within the physical environment, but most importantly a place in history. That's why we must consider the issue of time.

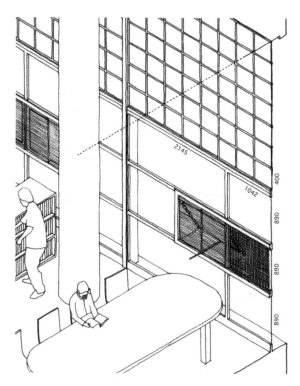

Biblioteca Central de la UNAM
Library / Mexico City, Mexico / Aw

メキシコの建築家ファン・オゴルマン設計の大学図書館。
直射日光が入りすぎないよう、上半分に薄い石板を嵌め
込み、光をにじませている。下半分のガラス窓は一部が
跳ね出し、通風を確保することができる。

66 光と風―にじみの窓

Figure I1.4
Biblioteca Central de la UNAM, Mexico City.
Photo and diagrams by Tokyo Institute of Technology, Graduate School
of Architecture and Building Engineering, Tsukamoto Laboratory

Part 2

Making:
A Framework for
Hands-On Work

Chapter 4
Imagery

Exercise: Making a Screen

What sources inspire ideas for an architecture design project?
Do the ideas visualized in your mind produce a design concept,
or do ideas visualized physically inform the design concept? What
are effective ways of imagining ideas? Through drawings? Sketches?
Models? What are the best ways to communicate your ideas
to others?

In groups of three or four, design a screen that provides shade
to a residence and solves overheating problems.

Pay close attention to (and hopefully discover) how imagery
can be used to develop the design. First, visualize your design
ideas mentally and physically through the act of making sketches,
diagrams, and models. Making sketches and models will allow you
to see how choices of materials can affect the functionality and
form of the screen. Next, explore and select actual images that
clearly convey your ideas and arrive at a consensus on which idea
to pursue. Then discuss what was discovered through Making, and
reflect the results of the discussion in the design. Repeat this cycle
of making, exploring images, discussing, and designing until the
screen design is finalized. Lastly, present an approximately 4-foot
by 8-foot full-scale mock-up of the screen.

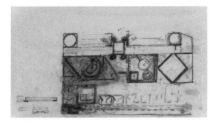

Figure 4.1
Louis I. Kahn (1902–1974),
Fine Arts Center, School and
Performing Arts Theater, Fort
Wayne, Indiana, site plan and
elevation sketches, 1963. Charcoal
and crayon on tracing paper,
12 × 22 in (30.5 × 55.9 cm).
Gift of the architect. The Museum of
Modern Art, New York, NY, U.S.A.

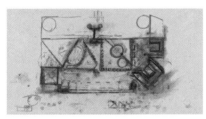

Figure 4.2
Louis I. Kahn (1902–1974),
Fine Arts Center, School and
Performing Arts Theater, Fort
Wayne, Indiana, site-plan sketch,
1963. Charcoal and crayon on
tracing paper, 12 × 22 in (30.5
× 55.9 cm).
Gift of the architect. The Museum of
Modern Art, New York, NY, U.S.A.

What is Imagery?

Imagery is the process of an architect seeking what he or
she wants to do in a design. Imagery can mean the mental
visualization of an idea for a design as well as the physical
visualization of the idea in a model or drawing. In addition
to creating imagery through visualization we can also use
pre-existing imagery, or actual pictures, to communicate and
clarify the design idea. There is a constant interplay between
these two different types of imagery. Imagery has a quality of
flexibility that allows the design concept to be pushed forward.
For example, sketching helps architects to both generate
and physically actualize mental pictures. In short, the act of
sketching may clarify ideas, or inspire new ideas which are in
turn reflected in the sketch.

Louis Kahn sometimes drew over and over with charcoal on a single sketch on tracing paper, for example in his sketches of the Fine Arts Center, School and Performing Arts Theater, Fort Wayne, Indiana (Figures 4.1 and 4.2). Some areas are so dark that it is hard to see what was first drawn, but this indicates Kahn's painstaking effort to visualize a project, as if looking for the form of the design within the overlapping lines.

Similarly, the countless study models made by Reiser + Umemoto demonstrate a search for an image that will drive a project (Figure 4.3).

Figure 4.3
Reiser + Umemoto. Study models
of Vector Wall.

Imagery in Design Development

Using the techniques of imagery, three groups of four students designed and constructed full-scale mock-ups of screens for Carraig Ridge Net Zero Passive House, a residence in the Canadian Rockies designed by Seattle-based firm Olson Kundig Architects (Figure 4.4). The architects were looking for inspiration to overcome shading and overheating issues, offering the students an opportunity to explore design through Making. In the Carraig Ridge house, the screen became a device for investigating tectonics and materials. The process of Making here was an act of inquiry, and imagery a key to design development.

Figure 4.4
Olson Kundig Architects, Carraig Ridge Net Zero Passive House. Perspective of the exterior view of the house.

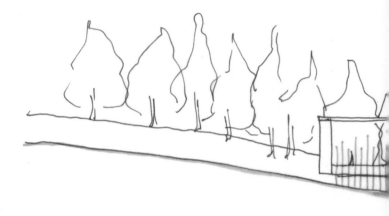

To start the design process, the students visualized ideas
for a screen and presented their ideas through sketches and
rough study models. After they had refined their visualizations,
Olson Kundig Architects asked them to present their design
ideas along with actual images that would more clearly
convey these ideas. Once the students in a group arrived at
a consensus on an idea, they continued refining the design.
During the process the design evolved along with the imagery.
At the end, the students made full-scale mock-ups of their

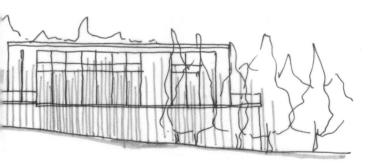

Figure 4.5
Alan Abdulkader, Katie Chapman,
Stephen Foster, and Laurissa Hale,
Folding Leaves. Elevation sketch of
glass rods idea.

final design solutions. The intent of the exercise was not for
the students to hold onto a single idea from beginning to end
but for them to repeatedly examine and question their design
through imagery.

During the early stages of *Folding Leaves* (2010), Alan
Abdulkader, Katie Chapman, Stephen Foster, and Laurissa
Hale visualized a series of glass rods planted on the south
face of the residence, constructed like a solar evacuated tube
filled with fluid (Figure 4.5). The sun would heat up the fluid

Figure 4.6
Olson Kundig Architects, Carraig Ridge House. Panorama photograph of the site.

Figure 4.7
Alan Abdulkader, Katie Chapman, Stephen Foster, and Laurissa Hale, *Folding Leaves*. Aspen leaf image.

Figure 4.8
Alan Abdulkader, Katie Chapman, Stephen Foster, and Laurissa Hale, *Folding Leaves*. Paper leaf study models.

and drive the core glass rods upward to act as a screen. The students connected their visualizations of linearity with trees and presented their idea to Olson Kundig using a photograph of aspen trees on the site (Figure 4.6). The screen came to be considered as an extension of the landscape.

Building on the image of trees, the next iteration was a series of paper leaves evenly spaced and stacked vertically at an optimum angle to block the sun (Figures 4.7 and 4.8). The leaves of the screen would be foldable in order to hide the screen, if desired (Figure 4.9). This idea was further developed by replacing the paper with Cor-ten steel and the folds with hinges. However, the hinges removed the elastic character of paper from the design. In order to build elasticity back into the screen, custom spring-loaded hinges were fabricated to make the steel behave like the paper. The screen still appeared too heavy and immovable, so the team tried using paper instead of steel, keeping the hinges (Figure 4.10). In the final mock-up, therefore, the team reverted to the folded paper (Figures 4.11–4.14). The idea of linearity and the aspen trees from the early stage of *Folding Leaves* provided the team with a common image to help determine the direction of the project.

With *Paper Compression Screen* (2010), Shona Bose, Monica DeGraffenreid, Lauren Kinker, and Laurie Nii approached the exercise very differently. Each team member mentally visualized the screen independently at first, then the team produced a number of study models and decided on the idea of compression as the basis for their screen design. They tested various materials that could facilitate compression, such as

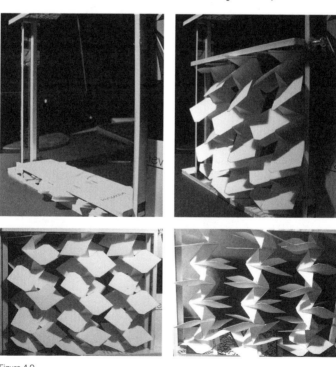

Figure 4.9
Alan Abdulkader, Katie Chapman, Stephen Foster, and Laurissa Hale, *Folding Leaves*. Stacked paper leaf study model.

Figure 4.10
Alan Abdulkader, Katie Chapman, Stephen Foster, and Laurissa Hale, *Folding Leaves*.
Mechanically hinged leaf study model.

Figure 4.11
Alan Abdulkader, Katie Chapman, Stephen
Foster, and Laurissa Hale, *Folding Leaves*.
Final mock-up.

Figure 4.12 (opposite)
Alan Abdulkader, Katie Chapman, Stephen
Foster, and Laurissa Hale, *Folding Leaves*.
Final mock-up detail.

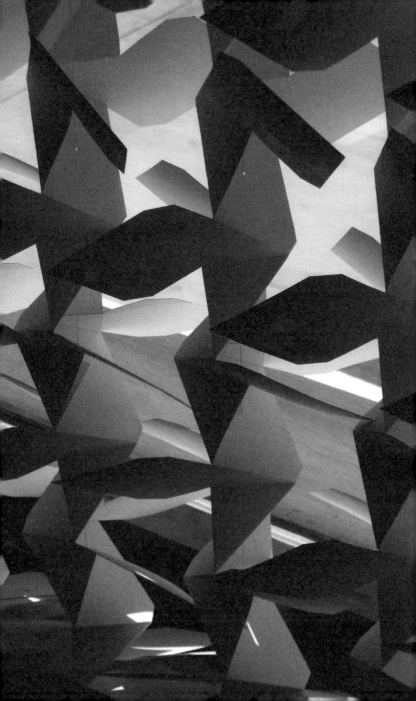

Figure 4.13
Alan Abdulkader, Katie Chapman, Stephen Foster, and Laurissa Hale, *Folding Leaves.* Exterior elevation.

Figure 4.14 (above)
Alan Abdulkader, Katie Chapman, Stephen Foster, and Laurissa Hale, *Folding Leaves.* View from interior.

Figure 4.15 (below)
Shona Bose, Monica DeGraffenreid, Lauren Kinker, and Laurie Nii, *Paper Compression Screen.* Study models for material testing.

marshmallows, gummy bears, fishing lures, umbrellas, and paper fans and lanterns. They made study models to examine which of the materials would have the proper elasticity to allow it to return to its original shape after being compressed (Figure 4.15).

Paper was found to have the best elasticity for this application. The team decided to use paper as a material that would open and close based on the image of an umbrella or a flower (Figures 4.16 and 4.17). The full-scale mock-up was made of 64 paper "flowers" assembled in a rectangular grid (Figure 4.18). The screen lets sunlight in when the flowers are closed and keeps it out when they are open. Each paper unit is manipulated by hand (Figure 4.19). To open a flower completely, a paper unit is pressed until it latches and remains open. Because they are connected with thread, when one flower is opened, the surrounding flowers open partially. However, each flower must be pressed and latched to completely open the paper units (Figures 4.20 and 4.21).

Figure 4.16
Shona Bose, Monica DeGraffenreid, Lauren Kinker, and Laurie Nii, *Paper Compression Screen.* Umbrella study models for material testing.

Part 2 Making: A Framework for Hands-On Work

Figure 4.17
Shona Bose, Monica DeGraffenreid, Lauren Kinker, and Laurie Nii,
Paper Compression Screen. Flower study models.

Figure 4.18 (opposite)
Shona Bose, Monica DeGraffenreid, Lauren Kinker, and Laurie Nii, *Paper Compression Screen*. Final mock-up.

Figure 4.19
Shona Bose, Monica DeGraffenreid, Lauren Kinker, and Laurie Nii. *Paper Compression Screen*. Final mock-up detail.

Figure 4.20
Shona Bose, Monica DeGraffenreid, Lauren
Kinker, and Laurie Nii, *Paper Compression
Screen*. Closed view from interior.

Figure 4.21
Shona Bose, Monica DeGraffenreid, Lauren
Kinker, and Laurie Nii, *Paper Compression
Screen.* Open view from interior.

Toyo Ito's Imagery

Architect Toyo Ito approaches design with a strong conceptual image. The essence of his architecture can be found in his visualization of a traditional Japanese *Manmaku* screen – a temporary cloth enclosure that loosely surrounds outdoor entertaining areas during cherry-blossom viewing. A sketch of Ito's mental visualization of *Manmaku* illustrates a loose and open boundary between outside and inside, a boundary that disappears completely after the party, when the curtain comes down and the space returns to nature (Figure 4.22).

Figure 4.22
Toyo Ito, *Manmaku* sketch.

This image of a fluid relationship between outside and inside is the foundation of Ito's architecture. Sometimes his building forms are blended into the landscape. Sometimes the interior space in his buildings looks like an extension of the exterior space. Ito vividly expresses the role of nature in his visualization of architecture: "When I draw an image of

Figure 4.23
Toyo Ito, Sendai Mediatheque. Exterior photo.

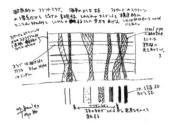

Figure 4.24
Toyo Ito, Sendai Mediatheque. Concept sketch. Notes in sketch: "(1) Completely flat slab, seaweed-like columns, screen facade, express only these three elements purely, study each element structurally, and simply them as much as possible, leave all the rest as a void. (2) Crossed steel pipe or punched holes on steel plate. (3) Include circulation cores or fitting. (4) Front gradation back, content of the columns varies from void to dense. (5) Thinnest slab, flat, random floor height. (6) Screen facade has only horizontal strips (with transparent or translucent film)."

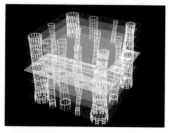

Figure 4.25
Toyo Ito, Sendai Mediatheque. Structural system computer graphic diagram showing plates, tubes, and skin.

what I think about architecture, I imagine natural elements such as gardens, woods, forests, and flow of water rather than a structural presence such as architecture."[1] He holds this imagery deep inside when he works on a project, but he does not use it directly – his design embodies it naturally.

For instance, Ito's design for Sendai Mediatheque (2001) blurs the border between inside and outside by rejecting the idea of spatial partitions or individual rooms and focusing instead on floor slabs, tube columns, and a screen facade (Figures 4.23–4.25). The tube columns originated from images of seaweed and of trees. The columns penetrate the floor slabs and obscure the boundaries between upper and lower floors and, according to Ito, create a spatial experience similar to walking through a forest (Figure 4.26).[2]

Ito is emphatic in his explanation of the critical importance of trees and nature to architecture:

The presence of trees creates different spaces among
which people can choose where to do whatever,
in much the same way as humans since ancient
times have made places to live within the flux of
nature. Long ago, the act of making a building used
to consist in creating relationships relative to this
natural flux, but architecture has long since cut
itself off from such fluidity and turned into a labor of
linking up closed rooms.[3]

Ito's primary image of *Manmaku* overlaps with his attempt
in Sendai Mediatheque to eliminate such separate rooms and
to open up the boundaries between the building and nature.

The Sendai Mediatheque sketch (Figure 4.24) is abstract,
but Ito's textual explanations in its margins clearly articulate
his concept. The term "seaweed-like" gives life to the columns
and clearly conveys the fluidity that Ito is seeking in the space.
Imagery therefore works as a metaphor by associating a design
element (columns) with an unrelated object (seaweed).

Imagery should not directly take the form of architecture,
rather it should guide architecture from abstract to concrete
design. That is, the image sparks creativity. It can also be used
as a means of communicating, critiquing, and evaluating in the
design process, and, as a metaphor, imagery has the power to
bring a poetic quality to design.

Figure 4.26
Toyo Ito, Sendai
Mediatheque.
Interior photo.

Chapter 5
Material Exploration

Exercise: Making an Enclosure

How do we get to know and understand materials? We can use our bodies to physically interact with materials: we can touch, bend, pound, roll, fold, cut, slice, press, and melt them. Another way to learn about materials is to research how they are made, possibly visiting a nearby manufacturer. Where did the materials come from? Are they shipped from far away, or can they be found nearby? Is the manufacturing process complex or simple? How has a particular material been used throughout history in different regions? We can come up with many questions about materials to study them. The investigations give rise to a new awareness of materials, and this awareness may be a source of design ideas.

After thinking about these general questions, study a common material frequently used in architectural applications: wood. Expand your knowledge of wood by manipulating it in different ways. For example, you might roll up a piece of veneer, stitch bark together, or carve blocks of wood.

Based on these investigations, design an enclosure and make a full-scale mock-up. The size and program of the enclosure should be dictated by the investigations.

Figure 5.1
Birch trees.

Materials as Initiators of Design

The purpose of this exercise is to help students think about
the relationship between materials and design. In the studio,
students present their designs through scaled drawings,
models, renderings, and so on. Because these are student
projects, actual buildings are not built, except in design-build
studios. Time is spent on conceptualization, program and
site analysis, and socio-cultural context, and then a building
is designed. Materials are often considered during or after
the design stage in a studio course, and rarely before.
Students draw up a building design or form on a computer
and then decide on materials by choosing between the various
options the program offers. The design is primary,
the materials secondary.

In the exercise presented here, the order was deliberately
reversed. The material was considered first, and after mapping
what they learned about the wood's materiality, the students
conceptualized, analyzed the context, and designed an
enclosure. Each student determined his or her own definition
of "enclosure" and selected a site to install the finished project.
The form of the enclosure was determined by the nature of
wood, and the site selection was informed by the design.

Nicole Reeves started *Birch Enclosure* (2007) with an
investigation of birch bark (Figure 5.1). She found that birch

Figure 5.2
Nicole Reeves, *Birch Enclosure*. Birch bark
sample study.

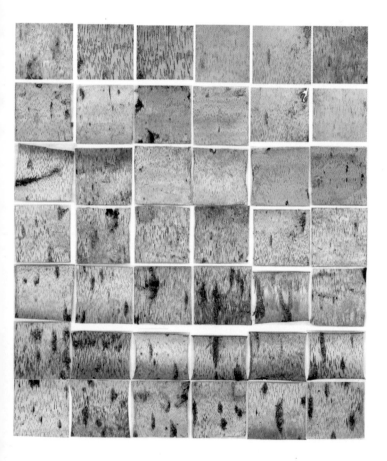

Figure 5.3
Nicole Reeves, *Birch Enclosure.* Exterior.

bark maintains a curved shape after it is stripped from the tree, that it is practically imperishable due to the fact that it contains a resinous oil, and that it is water resistant and offers good thermal insulation.

Reeves felt that the properties of birch bark meant it was a material that would lend itself to architectural applications, and wondered whether it had been used in architecture before. When she investigated, she discovered that birch bark had been an integral part of architecture in Finland, where it was used as moisture-proofing underneath board and sod roofs, between house foundations and walls, and to cover roofs.

Inspired by Finnish architecture, Reeves stitched together pieces of birch bark to make an enclosure with a form dictated by its curled nature (Figure 5.2). It was installed near a desk in a library to create a secluded space and to provide a layer of insulation from noise (Figures 5.3 and 5.4).

In *Containing Light / View* (2007), Matt Lamb investigated the properties of veneer, particularly its thinness, light transmittance, and structural potential. Lamb performed

Figure 5.4
Nicole Reeves, *Birch Enclosure*. Interior.

Figure 5.5
Matt Lamb, *Containing Light/View*. Veneer light study.

Figure 5.6
Matt Lamb, *Containing Light/View*.
Light-transmitting tubes.

Figure 5.7
Matt Lamb, *Containing Light/View*.
Final mock-up.

light and view studies using basswood veneer and found that light transmits through more than one layer of veneer (Figure 5.5). Instead of manipulating light transmittance with flat layers, he rolled up sheets of veneer to form light-transmitting tubes, which were assembled into an enclosure for collecting light (Figure 5.6). By varying the diameter of the tubes and assembling the tubes into different configurations, the pattern of light transmittance was more interesting than it would have been with flat sheets of veneer (Figure 5.7).

Material Exploration by Charles and Ray Eames in Design

Never has such a diverse array of materials been used in architecture as is employed now, and new materials continue to be introduced. This huge range of materials is categorized, distributed, and chosen by architects based on a number of considerations, including their performance, attributes, cost, and design application.

Historically, the choice of materials was limited to what was available locally. People living in forested regions would naturally cut trees for use in buildings, and people living in regions with many stones would likewise cut and carve stones for use. In places without trees or stones, sand would be mixed with water to make bricks.

Use of local materials diminished with the development of mass-produced materials after the Industrial Revolution. Looking to the innovative industrial materials developed during World War II, such as fiberglass, molded plywood, and synthetic resins, Charles and Ray Eames explored the design potential of mass-produced materials in their furniture and architecture. They designed four different chairs, one each of molded plywood, of fiberglass-reinforced plastic, of bent and welded wire-mesh, and of cast aluminum. The flexibility of these materials enabled the Eameses to design chairs that fit the human body perfectly (Figure 5.8). They further developed

Figure 5.8
Charles and Ray Eames, stack of
fiberglass-reinforced plastic chairs,
1954; dining armchair, produced
1950–1989.
Photo: Thomas Dix

Figure 5.9
Charles and Ray Eames, Eames House. Exterior.

Figure 5.10
Charles and Ray Eames, Eames House. Prefabricated steel sections.

design and fabrication techniques for molded plywood in their designs for leg splints, sculptures, and tables.

In the Eameses' own residence, the Case Study House #8 (the Eames House; 1949), they experimented with standard industrial materials and showed that even mass-produced materials could create good design (Figure 5.9). Instead of manipulating materials to produce custom-designed details, their design was based on the attributes of mass-produced materials that they selected from catalogs and assembled as a building. Ray Eames articulately explains the goal of using mass-produced materials: "It was the idea of using materials in a different way, materials that could be bought from a catalog. So that there was a continuation of the idea of mass production, so that people would not have to build stick by stick, but with material that comes ready-made – off-the-shelf in that sense."[1]

The Eames House was one of the first houses to use a prefabricated steel-frame structure (Figures 5.10 and 5.11). It consists of two light steel-framed rectangular boxes (house and studio) separated by a central court. The frame is subdivided by steel beams into bay modules that are 20 feet long, 7 feet 4 inches wide, and 17 feet high; the house is composed of eight bay modules and the studio of five. The court is the width of four bays. Each bay module is infilled with one or more industrial materials, such as painted plaster, plywood, asbestos, or glass. The prefabricated parts allowed the frame structure to be constructed by five workers in only sixteen hours. The Eames House demonstrated the benefits of a modular system and advanced the concept of a prefabricated components kit from which various home designs could be built. The Eames were able to demonstrate the flexibility of design that comes from exploring and understanding industrialized materials and construction methods.

Often, architects start with a general concept for a project, which then progresses gradually to specific material choices and details. However, sometimes reversing this direction stimulates ingenuity in design. Instead of starting design at the large scale and moving to the details, this chapter focused on beginning with the materials and details, and allowing the material behavior to lead to a final design solution.

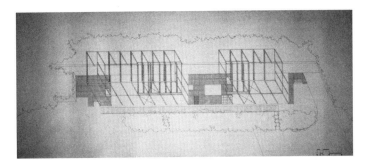

Figure 5.11
Charles and Ray Eames, Eames House. Axonometric drawing.

Chapter 6
Lag

Exercise: Making a Device for Perceiving Physical Movement

In the physical world, our bodies interact with buildings and the landscape. The interactions remain as marks or traces. The traces of collective movements can be witnessed in worn-out stair treads or on brass door handles made shiny through use. Our movements are imprinted in the architecture with which we interact.

Observe your physical movements in daily life. How does your arm move when you open a door? How do your feet move when you climb stairs? What differences can you observe when you open a heavy door, as opposed to a light door? Our bodies are able to perform complex movements naturally and easily in the context of our daily lives. Think consciously about how we accomplish these movements, with the aim of understanding the complexities.

Next, present these observations of your body by making a device that displays traces and patterns of your physical movement. An example might be a device that documents the movement of the arm rotating with the shoulder at the center: one could pound a nail into a wall at shoulder height, and tie a thread of arm's length to the nail and a pencil to the other end of the thread – the user of the device would hold the pencil and draw a circle on the wall. Mechanisms such as this allow us to observe and be aware of the relationship between the body and the environment.

Lag between Perception and Behavior

In order to perceive our environment, we move around and use our senses. Our senses are open to the environment. Our eyes recognize the environment visually, and the visual information allows us to navigate the environment. Our sense of touch also allows us to understand the environment: our bodies interact with materials in space, and by touching a material we can determine its identity – whether it is stone, metal, or wood. Our feet on the ground inform us about the nature of the materials we are standing on: a soft surface is more difficult to balance on than a hard surface; our feet touch and walk on a slope differently than on a flat surface – not only that, the posture of our entire body instinctively shifts to compensate for the angle of the slope. Even movements like spooning sugar into coffee or jumping over a puddle, which seem simple, are complex.

Science writer Tor Nørretranders explains one reason for this complexity in his book *The User Illusion* (1998):

> Every single second, millions of bits of information flood in through our senses. But our consciousness processes only perhaps forty bits a second – at most. Millions and millions of bits are condensed to a conscious experience that contains practically no information at all.[1]

We cannot consciously understand complex physical movements because, instead of being dictated by consciousness, they occur in direct response to sensory stimuli from the environment.

Another reason for the complexity of seemingly simple movements is the lag that arises between perception and behavior. An experiment by neuroscientist Benjamin Libet found that there is a half-second delay between the initiation of a movement and a (subsequent) conscious awareness of our intention to move.[2] Libet's findings indicate that we first

Figure 6.1
Michael Dale,
Sitting Field.
Bench and
switches.

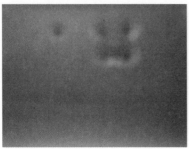
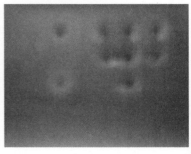

make decisions subconsciously – our belief that these decisions have been made consciously is due only to our retrospective perception of the experience.[3] The half-second delay, or lag, is thus disguised so that our experience of the world is fluid and not disjointed.

Even though our consciousness conceals lag of this type, we experience lag in other everyday situations. For example, if we prick our skin with a pin, there is a short delay before we feel pain. Spatially, too, when we move into a dark space from a bright space, it takes time for our eyes to adjust. Making a device for perceiving physical movement documents the relationships between perception and behavior, and environment and behavior, and can reveal lag.

Figure 6.2
Michael Dale, *Sitting Field*. Magnetic field patterns on magnetic film screen.

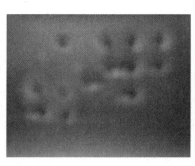

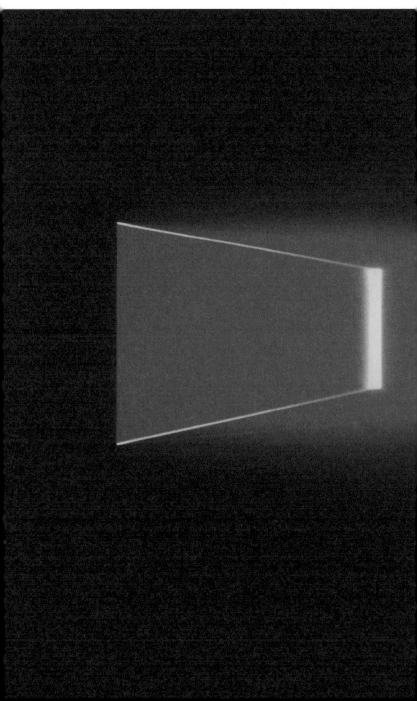

Figure 6.3
Milk Run, © James Turrell, 1996. Light projection of fluorescent tubes and colored gel, dimensions variable.
Photo: Lee Stalsworth

Lag in Design

Sitting Field (2006) by Michael Dale reveals the magnetic pattern of a body engaged in the act of sitting by imprinting it on a screen of magnetic film. The user sits on an array of switches installed on the surface of a bench (Figure 6.1). As the switches are depressed by the user's weight, they activate the corresponding electromagnets behind the magnetic film screen, creating a two-dimensional magnetic field pattern on the screen (Figure 6.2). The captured pattern differs depending on the position and duration of sitting. Thus different activities – such as reading a book or sitting with another person – are recorded as different patterns. A lag arises between the movement and the display of patterns. This lag is analogous to the lag between perception and behavior.

Artist James Turrell works with complex processes of light manipulation that produce a lag in visual perception. In *Milk Run* (1996), for example, visitors are guided into a completely dark room (Figure 6.3). At first, nothing is visible, but after approximately 15 minutes, a dim, red shape begins to appear. It is the illusion of a three-dimensional object floating in the corner of the room, created by a fluorescent light projected onto the two-dimensional walls from a hidden source.

Lag also can be experienced in the manipulation of light and space in architecture. The Southern Noh Stage at Nishi Honganji in Kyoto, Japan, was built in 1694 in a courtyard filled with white stones (Figure 6.4). As the visitors enter the space, they walk along the outside corridor looking at the stage while the white stones reflect sunlight into their eyes. Then they move into an enormous tatami room across the courtyard from the stage. The room is dim even during the day, because the wide eaves block the sunlight. Upon entering, visitors are not able to see the stage across the courtyard very well, but after their eyes adjust they can see the scenery painted on the stage. This lag not only physically and psychologically prepares visitors for a performance, but also clearly articulates the spatial experience as a journey from the outside corridor to the audience hall.

Figure 6.4
Southern Noh Stage at Nishi Honganji, Kyoto, Japan.
Photo: Taiji Miyasaka

The theme of lag caused by technology is present in projects by architects Elizabeth Diller and Ricardo Scofidio. In 1998 Diller and Scofidio, in collaboration with the Builder's Association, produced a multimedia theatrical performance entitled *Jet Lag*. The story is about a woman who kidnaps her grandson and travels with him back and forth from New York to Amsterdam 167 times over a period of six months in order to dodge the boy's father. After such frequent and continuous air travel, the grandmother dies of jet lag. In this case, "lag" is perceived as the result of physically moving from one place to another, and the result of extreme lag is death.

In 2000 Diller and Scofidio designed a restaurant called Brasserie in the Seagram Building, one of the most architecturally influential skyscrapers in New York City, designed by Mies van der Rohe and completed in 1958. When someone enters the restaurant through a revolving door, a sensor triggers a camera that snaps a time-lapse photo, which is displayed on one of the 15 monitors over the bar (Figure 6.5). The most recent snapshot takes the first position in the series of screens and displaces the previous ones to the right, dropping the oldest. Brasserie customers are not aware of the monitors at the entrance; only when they sit down do they see a snapshot of themselves on a monitor (Figure 6.6). Looking at the image on the monitor, the customers see themselves through someone else's eyes. A lag is generated between where they *were* (in the entry) and where they *are* (at a table or the bar). While lag is often regarded as something to be fixed or eliminated, Diller and Scofidio treated it here as a design opportunity.

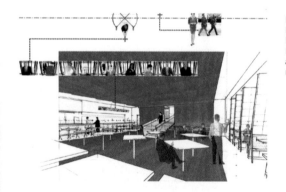

Figure 6.5
Diller Scofidio + Renfro, Brasserie, New York, NY. Plan and perspective rendering.

Figure 6.6
Diller Scofidio + Renfro, Brasserie, New York, NY. Photo of girl at bar.
Photo: Michael Moran/OTTO

Chapter 7
Geometric Scale

Exercise: Making a Cube

A cube, as a Platonic solid, is one of the purest geometric forms. In making a cube, we start by picturing the abstract geometric form in our thoughts. Then we must reify it. This exercise enables us to learn how scaling up can help in the concretization of the abstract.

First, find a cube in the environment. Is it a single, solid cube or composed of different elements? Does it consist of linear components or other parts? Do you need imaginary lines to define it, as do constellations of stars? Is the cube permanent or temporary? Does it have a smooth or rough surface, or no surface at all? What kind of edges does it have – smooth, rough, … ?

Next, make multiple 2-inch cubes. What materials can be used to make a cube? How can you use a material to make a cube? Do you press it? Cast it? Bind it? What material is most suitable for making a sharp-edged cube? What about a round-edged one?

After making a number of small cubes, put all of them on a table and divide them into groups based on categories that you define, such as soft, hard, porous, nonporous, light, or heavy.

Finally, construct a 3-foot cube. Think about the material, assembly systems (how to make the cube by assembling elements), and structure (how to make the cube support itself). Choose a site for your 3-foot cube by considering the relationship that you want the cube to have with the environment and the people who inhabit it.

Theoretical and Empirical Approaches to Geometry

There are two approaches to geometry as it pertains to architecture: theoretical and empirical. The theoretical approach employs a point, line, plane, or volume, as found in Cartesian coordinate space. This space exists in abstract thought but not in reality, because a point, line, plane, and volume have no weight or texture. Meanwhile, the empirical approach emphasizes perception of the geometric shapes found in reality, such as a round stool, a square table, or leaves. In certain instances, we can reconcile the theoretical approach with the empirical approach. For example, when we put a set square next to a column on the ground, we understand the meaning of an abstract right angle in the empirical sense.

In the design process, architects use the theoretical approach to envision a design idea. Then they draw geometric shapes in two dimensions and produce geometric forms as three-dimensional models. These ideas, drawings, and models then progress into real, concrete forms that can be experienced empirically. The theoretical and empirical approaches exist on an abstract–concrete continuum affected by scale. Theoretically, a geometric shape/form appears the same in all scales, but empirically, it looks different based on scale.

Scaling Up Based on Material Systems

Scaling up is one method of bringing reality to abstraction, because scaling up increases concreteness by enabling us to visualize the details more clearly. Washington State University students learned to navigate between small and large scale when designing and making their 2-inch and 3-foot cubes. The students used a variety of materials to make the 2-inch cubes, including paper, plastics, metal, wood, plaster, and stone, and even soap, lard, and salt. The methods of making the 2-inch cubes were also diverse: Plaster and lead were cast. Wood pieces were glued or screwed. Salt was pressed. Metal was cut.

When the students shifted to working on the 3-foot cubes, they had to use different materials and methods. For example it was possible to make a 2-inch cube out of lard, but it would be difficult to make a 3-foot version because it would be unlikely that the lard would be able to support its own weight. A 3-foot cube based on a 2-inch cube of assembled wood pieces connected with glue would require a stronger adhesive. A material's properties dictate how it will behave at different scales.

When making the 3-foot cube, therefore, the students needed to be more conscious of material behavior than when making a 2-inch cube. In *Earth Cube* (2008), Brandon Harris compressed soil to form a 3-foot cube (Figure 7.1). To make the cube, he had to understand the properties of the soil. If it contained too many aggregates or too much sand, it would not have stuck together when compressed.

For *Rope Cube* (2008), Angela Brackett devised a way of expressing a 3-foot cube without using any straight lines (Figure 7.2). A flexible material is required to make curved lines, but structural integrity is also necessary in order to make a self-standing cube. Brackett selected rope with which to create curved lines and hardened it by dipping it in resin (Figure 7.3). By understanding and using the materiality of the rope, Brackett found the right spacing between the curves to make a cube without using the outlines of a cube. If the

Figure 7.1
Brandon Harris, *Earth Cube.*

Figure 7.3
Angela Brackett, *Rope Cube*. Detail.

Figure 7.2
Angela Brackett, *Rope Cube*.

spacing between the rope paths was too wide, it would be difficult to perceive the cube as a whole; if the spacing was too narrow, it would be hard to control the curve of the rope. It was difficult at the beginning to imagine how the rope would form a cube, but Brackett's research on the properties of rope and her engagement with the rope's system of materiality enabled her to make one successfully.

In *Reflective Cube* (2008), Adam Pazan designed a cube without solid planes or edge lines (Figures 7.4 and 7.5). His goal was to challenge the definition of the cube as a solid mass by making a 3-foot cube using an assembly of vertical lines instead of six solid planes. The varying thicknesses of the lines reveal the volume of the cube. To achieve this, Pazan cut a roll of reflective Mylar into 900 long strips which were thin in the top and bottom thirds and thick in the middle third, where the cube is represented. These strips were hung from the ceiling. Each strip reflects the surroundings and reduces the materiality of the cube. The success of *Reflective Cube* depended on Pazan's understanding of how the individual strips of Mylar would come together as a whole.

Figure 7.4
Adam Pazan, *Reflective Cube.*

Figure 7.5
Adam Pazan,
Reflective Cube.
Detail.

Scaling Up Based on Structural Systems

In each of the student projects, the cubes were scaled up through the development of components, or details, which enabled the students to make a successful cube with a coherent design. Attention to the structural system when scaling up can also lead to good design, as architect Buckminster Fuller's work indicates. Fuller looked to nature's geometric patterns in order to find a structural system. He proposed that nature's geometry must be based on triangles:

> The triangle is a set of three energy events getting into critical proximity, so that each one with minimum effort stabilizes the opposite angle … Now, I found that a quadrilateral – a square, for example, – will not hold its shape. No rubber-jointed polygon holds its shape except one that is based on the triangle … I think all nature's structuring, associating, and patterning must be based on triangles, because there is not structural validity otherwise. This is nature's basic structure, and it is modellable … Now, if I'm going to subdivide the universe with triangles, how many triangles will it take to give me a system that will have both an inside and an outside? … I found that two triangles just fall back on each other and become congruent. I found that it takes a minimum of three triangles around a point. When you put in three triangles, with three common sides, around a point, they form a fourth triangle at the base and what you get is a tetrahedron. We know that nature always does things in the simplest and most efficient way, and structures based on tetrahedrons are the structures that nature uses … All the other shapes you find in nature are only transformable states of the tetrahedron."[1]

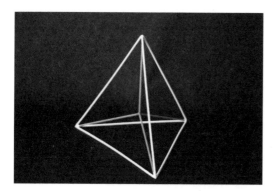

Figure 7.6
Buckminster Fuller,
Tetrahedron.
Fuller Artifacts
Box 12, Artifact
126, Buckminster
Fuller Collection,
Special Collections
Research Center,
Morris Library,
Southern Illinois
University
Carbondale.

By interlocking tetrahedrons (Figure 7.6) and icosahedrons, Fuller discovered that he could balance the forces of tension and compression, thereby distributing the loads evenly through a structure. Based on this discovery, Fuller designed the geodesic dome, in which he combined tetrahedrons to make a sphere. By continuing to add tetrahedrons, the geodesic dome can be scaled up indefinitely, and despite its low weight the total strength of the clear-span structure increases with size because of the synergetic forces at work. Of course, gravity affects the size and functions of the parts, but the structural system does not change.

Fuller built his first successful large geodesic dome building, called the Necklace Dome, in 1949 (Figure 7.7). It was constructed of aluminum aircraft tubing and a vinyl-plastic skin in the form of an icosahedron, 14 feet in diameter. Since then, thousands of large-scale geodesic domes have been built, using timber, plywood, metal, concrete, and other materials. Fuller's U.S. Pavilion at the International Exposition, Montreal, Canada (1967) is an exemplar (Figures 7.8 and 7.9). 206 feet in height and 250 feet in diameter, the structure of the Pavilion consists of two spheres, one nested in the other, with about three feet between them. The outer sphere is made of triangles, and the inner sphere is made of hexagons, which are connected by steel tubes, thus creating a structure of tetrahedrons.

Figure 7.7
Buckminster Fuller, Necklace Dome.

Figure 7.8
Buckminster Fuller,
Montreal Expo '67 Dome, exterior.

In his geodesic domes Fuller realized nature's structural principles as physical forms. He used tension and compression components to scale up and concretize the abstract structure of tetrahedrons found in nature. His tetrahedral geometries were "empirical structures flowing from microcosm to macrocosm."[2]

Architects are constantly navigating between theoretical and empirical worlds, between small scale and large scale, because architecture design generally starts from an abstract idea that must be developed and given a physical form. Working with geometric scale – scaling up in this exercise – brings a design idea into reality by demanding that consideration be given to the details of material and structural systems. Scaling up is a method by which architects are able to concretize the abstract and visualize details more clearly as progress is made toward the final design solution.

Figure 7.9 (opposite)
Buckminster Fuller, Montreal Expo '67 Dome. Interior detail.

Nanako Umemoto, Reiser + Umemoto, New York

Reiser + Umemoto is a multidisciplinary design office known for its innovative architecture, forward-thinking research, and experimentation through design. Throughout their work Jesse Reiser and Nanako Umemoto generate form by exploring the potential of materials and forces through Making.

Taiji Miyasaka: Your office makes physical and computer models as a tool to generate design. Can you explain more about the role of physical and computer models in your design process?

Jesse Reiser: Models shouldn't be taken out of the context of other ways of working. In other words, as a starting point, we would already assume that a physical model is in play, drawings are in play, programmatic diagrams might be in play, too. A series of models and methods are worked up simultaneously. Depending upon the situation, one may start with any of those, and one advances the project by entering into, say, the model making. Then there will be a point, however, in physical model making where it ceases to be a useful tool. For instance, it might have been generated without a stable notion of scale, so in order to advance the model, one would shift to a more measured drawing or projection. Then one would draw the model, change it, scale it, make the modifications that could be made in that other representation, and do a new model on the basis of the changes in the drawing. Most of the time, we don't detach the model from other tools, but rather circulate among the tools to advance a project.

Nanako Umemoto: Generally, one would never be able to generate the project totally from drawings, or totally by model making, or totally from 3D computer models. There is always this kind of dance among all of the different methods.

JR: There's no priority in that respect, either, in terms of the representational system or the scale. The typical method among architects is to work from a general scheme down to particular details, whereas we may actually work from extremely detailed conditions early on and have them fold back into the general scheme.

TM: Do you start strategizing right at the beginning of a project?

JR: Yes. It's never a single linear method, but actually a series of representation methods that get worked together. Typically, we exhaust the possibilities of one method, and then we go on to the next, which actually opens up the previous level. It is a productive way of advancing a project.

NU: We used to work on models, drawings, and programs linearly. We would work on a model and then shift to drawings, or vice versa. Of course, there were overlaps and exchanges among them, but now computers are so advanced that we can work on various things simultaneously, such as making physical and computer models, drawings, and whatever is necessary for the design process.

TM: To what extent can you anticipate the design direction from making models?

JR: Realistically, we have a general notion of where the project will go. It's not like a black box where we are inputting information. Some things happen that are unanticipated, things that one can't predict, and then the project changes as a consequence. A lot of times

Figure 12.1
Reiser + Umemoto, O-14 Tower.

there's more of a psychological aspect where you have an obsessive interest in trying to do some form of architecture, and then all of the other factors are pushing back against it to such an extent that you finally abandon it or make a major change. So it's never what you thought it was when you started.

NU: Yes, it doesn't come from a zero point. It comes from revisiting old ideas in a new form.

JR: Or it's about advancing a project to a certain point and then trying to find a new direction. For example, the connection between the O-14 Tower project in Dubai and the Shenzhen Airport project in China was extremely strong (Figure I2.1). There were interests in developing a concrete shell in O-14, and its fenestration and many other ideas got pulled into the airport proposal (Figure I2.2). We literally took the articulations that we were working on in a vertical structure and began working on it horizontally, and then upped the ante in the geometry by not just dealing with holes cut normal to the surface, but experimenting with a range of cuts that were oblique. These two projects are very tied to one another in terms of advancing certain directions.

Figure I2.2
Reiser + Umemoto, Shenzhen Airport.
Interior perspective.

Figure I2.3
Reiser + Umemoto, Aeon Tower.

NU: Also, it wasn't a linear development from the O-14 Tower to the airport. In fact, the O-14 Tower came from when we were developing the Aeon Tower in Dubai, which is an 85-story building (Figure I2.3). Our client was intrigued by our design and asked us to design a similar building of 22 stories. However, when we tried to create a similar building design at that small scale, the geometry of glass and mullions became so complex that it was physically impossible to design a similar building.

JR: We couldn't organize office spaces by simply reducing the scale of the form of the Aeon project.

NU: Suddenly we had to shift our approach to the design.

TM: The change in scale led to a shift in materiality as well.

JR: Totally. It went from a frame project to a shell project.

NU: Essentially, the structural core went outside and the mullions went inside (Figure I2.4).

Figure I2.4
Reiser + Umemoto, O-14 Tower model.

JR: There was a radical break in the middle of the project, from a glass-skin building to an exoskeleton. There was a vestigial aspect of the form. The form of the overall building in the first project was much more complex. The idea was that there would be a cruciform zone at the top of the tower for duplex apartments. The arms of the cross would allow for every apartment to have three exposures, and then the folds would open up and expand outward to house office space in the lower stories. That residential component was eliminated by the developer because of market changes, and the tower became all office space. However, we clung to a vestigial cruciform; it became a much fatter cross shape – a soft cruciform – to accommodate offices. It was ironic that the function of the cruciform in the original scheme was residential, and it was the only persistent feature of the original scheme in the final building, which is all offices. The function of the cruciform went from being predominantly programmatic in the early version to predominantly structural in the final.

TM: What were the main factors that determined these radical changes? For example, the design of the openings seems to be crucial in the O-14 Tower. How did the design of the holes change?

JR: At first, we proposed a horizontal-vertical diagrid, but the structural engineer found that this would not have worked structurally, although it would have worked as a pseudostructure, a kind of Vierendeel frame, which is not very structural, but basically a fairly inefficient rigid frame. We turned that grid on the diagonal, and then suddenly it started working like a shell, and luckily it was much more desirable aesthetically to do the diagonal as well. The vertical-horizontal orientation, which the builder at one point was pushing for, was not successful in our judgment, on either a structural or purely aesthetic level, so it was very nice that the diagrid worked both aesthetically and performatively.

TM: Is each of the holes different?

JR: There are five different sizes on anywhere there is a pure geometry. But then there are transitional zones between flat and

Figure I2.5
Reiser + Umemoto, Diagram I of O-14
Tower holes.

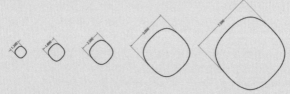

Figure I2.6
Reiser + Umemoto, Diagram II of O-14
Tower holes.

curved where a hole might lie over the two, so you get strangely shaped holes. Also, they shift and drift in the grid, so there are subtle differences of the size of the holes, even within one zone, which results in an enormous variety (Figure I2.5 and I2.6).

TM: I'm interested in your use of wax models in the design process (Figure I2.7). Wax is a unique material for architecture models. How did you start using wax?

JR: That was an accident of history. The wax that we first got had been used by sculptor Carl Milles at Cranbrook Academy of Art in Michigan. Sculptors were no longer doing wax casting, so there was an availability of this material. Architects started using it instead.

TM: How would you describe the uniqueness, or the advantages, of using a wax model?

JR: I usually say it stands halfway between a rigid model, like chipboard, and clay. It's flexible enough, but not too flexible. It has a plasticity that allows you to work quickly.

NU: For example, chipboard requires many layers to be used, and it is a very difficult material to cut, so it is wasteful.

TM: You can recycle wax immediately.

JR: That's right. I also think that the importance of the speed is a major factor. The models can be done very fast, and this allows

Figure I2.7
Reiser + Umemoto, wax models.

you to almost sketch three dimensionally, but with a real scale, which is part of the drawback of solely looking at the material in the computer and the perspective window. You can also never really see the true scale of relationships there. It is always distorted. With a 3D computer model, you have to constantly do output to inspect it as a dimensional thing. Otherwise you are surprised in a negative way. Maybe most people don't care, maybe some people don't even know the difference, but I think it is a huge problem. The wax is actually very useful in that it is fast; it allows you to do a metrical thing that can be evaluated in all aspects. If you are going to design with models, it takes so long to build in the first place that there is no inclination to change it, so wax is extremely helpful in this respect.

TM: Are wax models used equally with computer models, or is priority placed on wax models over computer models?

JR: There is no priority. It is done in a purely pragmatic way. There is no ideological bias, and it is just whatever works. It is purely a pragmatic assessment.

TM: Do you do much sketching to generate design?

JR: We do sketching also. Actually, the sketching for the most part is less three dimensional and more used to correct a 3D computer model. We evaluate mainly in 2D, and so I do a lot of sketching to change contours and make very subtle changes. I am constantly sketching, actually.

I've read similar stories about the Einstein Tower in Potsdam, Germany, too; there were hundreds of plan cuts done in 2D to make the 3D form. Gaudí did something similar, where even though he seems to be a sculptural architect, the way of developing and refining was about many, many 2D evaluations of profile. We mainly see the world flat. All evaluations are done flat while continuing to change one's position. I think it's a sculptural technique, actually. I would guess that even Michelangelo's sculptures were probably evaluated in the flat and against a 2D profile that was constantly changed and shifted. It's done when every aspect in space resolves itself perfectly as a 2D resolution. That's how I would do it.

TM: Perhaps this is related to our perception.

JR: I think so. It's also about process; it's about horizons. In order to correct anything, you can't correct all over. There's got to be a simpler way of breaking down a complex problem. It is about constantly evaluating the edge. But every evaluation has to be a simpler one, a 2D one, whereas machines do it indifferently to whatever is being produced.

TM: In that sense the computer is a very effective and useful tool.

JR: Yeah. It deals with all of those problems of building, or drawing or printing, by applying a Cartesian system to what might be a more complex physical reality. It is a way of taking something and analytically reproducing it, like a print bed moving up and down. Computers also could be used afterwards to discipline the form.

NU: Computers can be generative up to a point, but educated judgment by the architect is essential. There is no design without judgment; architecture is not automatic. Of course, computers are very good at analyzing what has already been designed.

TM: How does your office use manual model-making techniques alongside highly advanced computer modeling?

NU: We find out quite a lot of information after physically making models. As a matter of fact, there are certain models here that people think were done by a laser cutter, but they are actually hand cut. For example, the Vector Wall project for the Home Delivery show by Barry Bergdoll in 2008 at the Museum of Modern Art was modeled in the computer, but then it was printed out flat and hand cut. Until we deformed the sheet by hand, we didn't know how the openings would behave (Figure 12.8).

Figure I2.8
Reiser + Umemoto, Vector Wall model.

Part 2 Making: A Framework for Hands-On Work

JR: This is the prototype model of the project (Figure l2.9). This dealt with the feedback between the pattern that would be generated in a drawing and the physical deformation of a material, which is based in this case upon the model of expanded sheet metal, like plaster lath. A provisional pattern was generated knowing what a normative uniform stretch of a piece of material would do, and then the first patterns could be modified parametrically, for example by changing the length, changing the angle, changing the direction of the pattern and what its consequences would be formally when forces were applied to it. However, it's not something that one could easily emulate in the computer. One could do the pattern, but couldn't really emulate the true behavior of sheet metal and what it would do when forces were applied to it. Paper, though, would be a very close analog; cutting the paper pattern and pulling on it would essentially correspond to what steel would do. One could conceivably set up a robot that would be able to apply the forces to the right place on the sheet to produce those forms. However, the overall form and the adjustment of the pattern would be problematic for a robot to achieve, as the forces must literally be indexed by incremental adjustment of the sheet relative to the tool. It would be very hard to automate the process with the current technology.

NU: A fabricator tried it and then realized it would be impossible to do.

JR: Right. Actually, they did do the scaling up and cutting of the pattern in laser-cut steel, but then there were no machines that could expand the sheet steel properly, so it was actually done in reverse. We literally had to take screwdrivers and deform each cut, then manage the deformations, to get the steel to move into the proper form. So in the end we had to locally expand the cuts one by one in order to simulate external pulls on the surface. Of course, the final form is what we were after and how the forces arrived in the material was a secondary consideration.

TM: So you started to understand how the material would react.

Figure I2.9
Reiser + Umemoto, Vector Wall.

JR: Yes. But it is very hard to predict material behaviors while we are working. You go from the graphical pattern, and you sort of have a general hunch of how it's going to behave, but it is always different from what you thought. And then you have to adjust the pattern again, so it's iterative.

NU: We always make a significant number of models to study the behavior of materials. In this case, we tried different ways of cutting. For example, when we changed the angle slightly or changed the length of the cut, each field began to behave differently. Each field affects the others, so we couldn't guess what would really happen in terms of the overall behavior.

TM: Was the computer involved in this process?

NU: We actually tried to use the computer and then realized it would be impossible, because the surface would stretch in the computer. It was too flexible; it didn't have the constraints that the actual material had.

TM: Is it typical for you to generate design in reaction to material behavior?

JR: This is an extreme example because we were designing *and* making, whereas most architecture is more distant from this looping system. I think the models that we make work through those material issues, but then we generate something to be built by others remotely, so there is a different type of protocol involved.

TM: It is the architect's job to decide whether hand work is necessary or whether to integrate automatic production, but instead of considering handcrafting and computer production as independent from each other, it may be beneficial to think of them as seamlessly connected.

JR: Right. Instead of thinking of the human and the machine separately in the design process, just think about it as one thing. Whatever works pragmatically is important. But then finally the design has to get converted into a mechanical protocol, because it leaves your hands and it has to be industrially produced, unless you have teams of craftsmen. In Dubai we actually did have craftsmen, but their role was more to correct mistakes which occurred from the machines. That is part of the irony. The project is very early in the use of computation through the building process, and so there are utopian aspirations for a seamless model, and then there is the reality of what happens.

TM: How did the use of computation work in actual construction?

JR: There was a learning curve in the actual construction, because the capacity of the form work under the pressure of the concrete was never taken into account. The forms were cut perfectly, but then the pressure of the concrete at the bottom of each pour was such that they deformed the openings. The foam formwork actually got crushed from the pressure of the concrete, so the first stories had really misshapen openings, which then had to be ground back by hand.

NU: The drawings definitely show a diamond shape, but the workmen ground the openings to a perfectly round shape.

JR: There were some that they ground to look like arches, too! The contractor finally solved the problem by wrapping the edges of the molds with laminate, and that hardened them enough to withstand the pressure. They also had to figure out how to place the forms. These things are not a part of a normal routine for the builder, as there was no precedent in typical building practice.

TM: Do you often have to visit the construction site to solve problems with materials?

JR: I think it's almost too late in a project like that, but if you have to, you do.

NU: These are things you couldn't guess would happen. We thought we had considered every aspect of construction, but still these things happened.

JR: It was a material behavior which was unanticipated by everyone, including the engineers. They just didn't think of it. Maybe the foam-board that the contractor ordered didn't have a high enough capacity.

TM: I think this story is enlightening, especially for students, because they don't anticipate this type of difficulty with changing when they are in school, and in the studio culture they always try to figure out everything at the beginning.

NU: That's impossible. It is more like martial arts, where you have a battery of techniques, but the situations are constantly changing, so you have to respond to the unforeseen.

Pedagogy

TM: Both of you have been teaching in universities for a long time, including not only studios, but also workshops. Some architecture workshops are more generally focused on designing buildings, for example a public library, but it seems that your workshops have focused on Making.

NU: Yes, we usually have only five days to get the students to produce something.

JR: Typically the projects aren't ambitious in terms of programmatic complexity. We wouldn't ask them to do a theater complex, for example. We typically try to simplify the project, like a pavilion or a piece of furniture or a tent. It is the smallest example that could represent a certain direction of architectural thinking, the simplest version of what could become a much bigger architectural idea. The other aspect is that typically the ambitions might exceed the scale of the project. For example, the Aalto pavilion at the Venice Biennale points toward much larger buildings that he is thinking about, but it is the smallest structure that would represent that set of thoughts. Then you see more elaborate versions of it in much more permanent and complex projects.

TM: It becomes a prototype.

JR: Yeah, even if it's not the same program or the same scale. The Miesian model is really interesting, too. For example, his clear-span projects are first worked out at the scale of houses, but then he will have a middle-scale version and a grand version, too. He typically worked through three different scales of the same model irrespective of program.

TM: You also have students work a lot in one-to-one scale. Why is one-to-one scale important?

JR: I think it brings into play all of the elements that you would encounter in an architectural problem in the most direct or tangible way. They learn all of the conventions, too, in the simplest ways. They go through an analytical exercise; they basically learn how to think three dimensionally. To start, I give the students a car body to analyze. This year I moved away from the car model, and they all had to choose dolls instead. They would do systematic cross-sections, reconstruct the doll in another scale, and then go on to pattern making.

NU: Then they put the pattern together to make it three-dimensional again, but it ends up completely different from the original doll (Figure 12.10).

JR: Yeah, it's like designing shoes where the material dictates the flexibility, and thus there is a direct relationship between the simplicity or complexity of the pattern and its geometry.

They had to use calipers and transfer the measurements to profiles, and then the profiles got turned into a profile model, so they couldn't cheat. The model would then be compared to the original doll to see if they were making mistakes, so they had to learn how to work precisely, transfer, and rescale, and then they learned how to make a pattern to fit the skeleton.

TM: That is very interesting.

JR: Then I had them go on to the design of a piece of furniture, because they had the skills to think through the creation of a skeleton and a skin.

TM: That exercise is very different from assigning a project and having students come up with a big concept.

JR: Right. They learn technique. It's better to have technique. Then you can start thinking through technique. I remember Paul Valéry wrote that the real poets think through technique, not through emotions or concepts. It's much more than merely being a good technician. You know a professional because they are thinking through their technique.

Figure 12.10
Reiser + Umemoto,
example of analytical
doll exercise.

Notes

Introduction

1. Louis Kahn, as quoted in David B. Brownlee and David G. De Long, *Louis I. Kahn: In the Realm of Architecture* (London: Thames & Hudson, 1997), 110.
2. Samuel H. Scudder, "How Agassiz Taught Professor Scudder," in Lane Cooper (ed.), *Louis Agassiz as a Teacher: Illustrative Extracts on His Method of Instruction* (Ithaca, NY: The Comstock Publishing Co., 1917), 40–48.
3. Gregory Bateson, *Steps to an Ecology of Mind* (Chicago and London: The University of Chicago Press, 1972), 464–465.

Chapter 1

1. James Corner, "The Agency of Mapping: Speculation, Critique and Invention," in Denis Cosgrove (ed.), *Mappings* (London: Reaktion Books Ltd., 1999), 217.
2. Edward R. Tufte, *Visual Explanations* (Cheshire: Graphics Press, 1997), 9.
3. *Babylonian Map of the World*, BM 92687, British Museum, London.
4. D.W. Meinig, "The Beholding Eye: Ten Versions of the Same Scene," in D.W. Meinig (ed.), *The Interpretation of Ordinary Landscapes: Geographical Essays* (New York and Oxford: University Press, 1979), 33–34.
5. Art21, "Roni Horn: Water." http://www.art21.org/texts/roni-horn/interview-roni-horn-water
6. Bernard Rudofsky, *The Prodigious Builders: Notes Toward a Natural History of Architecture with Special Regard to those Species that are Traditionally Neglected or Downright Ignored* (New York and London: Harcourt Brace Jovanovich, 1977).
7. Peter Cook, *Experimental Architecture* (New York: Universe Books, 1970), 90.
8. See Peter Cook, *Archigram* (New York: Princeton Architectural Press, 1999).
9. Momoyo Kaijima, Junzo Kuroda, and Yoshiharu Tsukamoto, *Made in Tokyo* (Tokyo: Kajima Institute Publishing Co., Ltd., 2001), 9.
10. Quoted in Alexandra Tyng, *Beginnings: Louis I. Kahn's Philosophy of Architecture* (New York: Wiley & Sons, 1984), 171.
11. Beatriz Colomina, *Privacy and Publicity: Modern Architecture as Mass Media* (Cambridge, MA and London: The MIT Press, 1996), 118–119.
12. Walter Benjamin, *Selected Writings Volume 2, Part 2, 1931–1934,* ed. Michael W. Jennings et al., trans. Rodney Livingstone et al., (Cambridge: Belknap Press of Harvard University Press, 2005), 510.
13. In *Karl Blossfeldt Working Collages,* ed. Ann Wilde and Jürgen Wilde, trans. Christopher Jenkin-Jones (Cambridge, MA: The MIT Press, 2001), 12.
14. In Catherine Hürzeler, "Collaboration with Artists: Interview with Jacques Herzog," in *Herzog & de Meuron. Urban Projects. Collaboration with Artists. Three Current Projects* (Tokyo: TN Probe Toriizaka Networking, 1997), 63–64.
15. Ibid., 67.
16. Ibid., 99.

Chapter 3

1. Daniel Libeskind, *Daniel Libeskind: The Space of Encounter* (New York: Universe Publishing, 2000), 26–28.
2. Ibid.
3. Daniel Libeskind, *Breaking Ground: An Immigrant's Journey from Poland to Ground Zero* (New York: Riverhead Books, 2004), 56–57.
4. Ibid., 83.

Interview 1

1 Momoyo Kaijima, Junzo Kuroda, and Yoshiharu Tsukamoto, *Made in Tokyo* (Tokyo: Kajima Institute Publishing Co., Ltd., 2001).
2 Yoshiharu Tsukamoto, *WindowScape: Window Behaviourology* (Singapore: Page One, 2012).
3 Atelier Bow-Wow, *Pet Architecture Guide Book Vol. 2* (Tokyo: World Photo Press, 2002).

Chapter 4

1 Author's translation from Toyo Ito, *Tōsō suru kenchiku* (Tokyo: Seidosha, 2000), 339.
2 Toyo Ito, *Sendai Mediatheque*, eds. Tomoko Sakamoto and Albert Ferré (Barcelona: Actar, 2003), 15.
3 Ibid., 15.

Chapter 5

1 Oral History Interview with Ray Eames, July 28–August 20, 1980, Archives of American Art, Smithsonian Institution.

Chapter 6

1 Tor Nørretranders, *The User Illusion: Cutting Consciousness Down to Size* (New York: Viking Penguin, 1998), 125.
2 Libet conducted an experiment in the 1980s in which he asked subjects to choose at random a moment to flick their wrist while he measured the associated build-up of electrical signal, called the "readiness potential," in the brain. Libet wanted to know how the readiness potential corresponded to the felt intention to move. To determine when subjects felt the intention to move, he asked them to watch the second hand of a clock and report its position when they perceived that they had felt the conscious will to move. Libet found that the *unconscious* brain activity building up to the *conscious* decision by the subject to flick their wrist began approximately half a second *before* the subject consciously felt that they had decided to move. Benjamin Libet et al., "Time of Conscious Intention to Act in Relation to Onset of Cerebral Activity (Readiness-Potential): The Unconscious Initiation of a Freely Voluntary Act," *Brain* 106, no. 3 (1983): 623–642.
3 Benjamin Libet, "Unconscious Cerebral Initiative and the Role of Conscious Will in Voluntary Action," *Behavioral and Brain Sciences* 8, no. 4 (December 1985): 529–566.

Chapter 7

1 In Calvin Tomkins, "Profiles: In the Outlaw Area," *The New Yorker* 41, no. 47 (January 8, 1966): 54.
2 K. Michael Hays, "Fuller's Geological Engagements With Architecture," in Michael Hays and Dana Miller (eds.), *Buckminster Fuller: Starting With the Universe* (New York: Whitney Museum of American Art, and New Haven: Yale University Press, 2008), 11.

Selected Bibliography

Alexander, Christopher. *Notes on the Synthesis of Form.* Cambridge, MA: Harvard University Press, 1964.

Architectures of Herzog & de Meuron. Portraits by Thomas Ruff. Exh. Cat., *Herzog & de Meuron.* Peter Blum Gallery, New York, Summer 1994. New York: Peter Blum, 1995.

Arnheim, Rudolf. *The Dynamics of Architectural Form.* Berkeley and Los Angeles: University of California Press, 1977.

Atelier Bow-Wow. *Pet Architecture Guide Book Vol. 2.* Tokyo: World Photo Press, 2002.

Atelier Bow-Wow. *Echo of Space/Space of Echo.* Tokyo: INAX Publishing, 2009.

Baker, Geoffrey H. *Le Corbusier – The Creative Search: The Formative Years of Charles-Edouard Jeanneret.* London: E. & F.N. Spon, 1996.

Baird, Davis. *Thing Knowledge: A Philosophy of Scientific Instruments.* Berkeley and Los Angeles: University of California Press, 2004.

Balmond, Cecil. *Element.* London: Prestel Publishing Ltd., 2007.

Banham, Reyner. *The Architecture of the Well-Tempered Environment.* Chicago: The University of Chicago Press, 1969.

Bateson, Gregory. *Steps to an Ecology of Mind.* Chicago and London: The University of Chicago Press, 1972.

Bateson, Gregory. *Mind and Nature: A Necessary Unity.* Cresskill: Hampton Press, Inc., 2002.

Beck, Haig, and Jackie Cooper. *Glenn Murcutt: A Singular Architectural Practice.* Victoria: The Images Publishing Group Pty. Ltd., 2002.

Benjamin, Walter. *Selected Writings Volume 2, Part 2, 1931–1934,* eds Michael W. Jennings et al., trans. Rodney Livingstone et al. Cambridge, MA: Belknap Press of Harvard University Press, 2005.

Borges, Jorge Luis. *Collected Fictions,* trans. Andrew Hurley. New York: Viking, 1998.

Brooks, Rodney A. *Cambrian Intelligence: The Early History of the New AI.* Cambridge, MA and London: The MIT Press, 1999.

Brownlee, David B., and David G. De Long. *Louis I. Kahn: In the Realm of Architecture.* London: Thames & Hudson Ltd., 1997.

Colomina, Beatriz. *Privacy and Publicity: Modern Architecture as Mass Media.* Cambridge, MA and London: The MIT Press, 1996.

Cook, Peter. *Experimental Architecture.* New York: Universe Books, 1970.

Cook, Peter, ed. *Archigram.* New York: Princeton Architectural Press, 1999.

Cooper, Lane, ed. *Louis Agassiz as a Teacher: Illustrative Extracts on His Method of Instruction.* Ithaca, NY: The Cornstock Publishing Co., 1917.

Cosgrove, Denis, ed. *Mappings.* London: Reaktion Books Ltd., 1999.

Demetrios, Eames. *An Eames Primer.* New York: Universe Publishing, 2001.

Diller, Elizabeth, and Ricardo Scofidio. *Flesh: Architectural Probes.* New York: Princeton Architectural Press, 1994.

Forty, Adrian. *Words and Buildings: Vocabulary of Modern Architecture.* New York: Thames & Hudson, 2000.

Fried, Michael. *Why Photography Matters as Art as Never Before.* New Haven and London: Yale University Press, 2008.

Fuller, R. Buckminster. *Operating Manual for Spaceship Earth.* Baden: Lars Müller Publishers, 1969a.

Fuller, R. Buckminster. *Utopia or Oblivion: The Prospects for Humanity.* New York: Bantam Book, 1969b.

Fuller, R. Buckminster. *Critical Path.* New York: St. Martin's Press, 1981.

Gibson, James J. *The Ecological Approach to Visual Perception.* Boston: Houghton Mifflin Co., 1979.

Gombrich, E. H. *The Sense of Order: A Study in the Psychology of Decorative Art.* London: Phaidon Press, 1979.

Gorman, Michael John. *Buckminster Fuller: Designing for Mobility.* Milan: Skira Editore, 2005.

Hays, K. Michael, and Dana Miller, eds. *Buckminster Fuller: Starting with the Universe.* New York: The Whitney Museum of American Art, and New Haven: Yale University Press, 2008.

Hejduk, John. *Victims.* London: Architectural Association,1996.

Herzog, Jacques, Philip Ursprung, and Jeff Wall. *Pictures of Architecture, Architecture of Pictures: A Conversation Between Jacques Herzog and Jeff Wall, Moderated by Philip Ursprung,* ed. Christina Bechtler. Vienna and New York: Springer, 2004.

Horn, Roni. *Another Water: The River Thames, for Example.* Zurich, Berlin and New York: Scalo, 2000.

Horn, Roni. *Dictionary of Water.* Paris: Edition 7L, 2001.

Horn, Roni. *Weather Reports You.* London and Göttingen: Steidl & Artangel, 2007.

Ito, Toyo. *Toyo Ito Recent Project.* Tokyo: A.D.A. Edita Tokyo, 2008.

Ito, Toyo. *Sendai Mediateque.* eds. Tomoko Sakamoto and Albert Ferré. Barcelona: Actar, 2003.

Ito, Toyo. *Tōsō suru kenchiku.* Tokyo: Seidosha, 2000.

Kaijima, Momoyo, Junzo Kuroda, and Yoshiharu Tsukamoto. *Made in Tokyo.* Tokyo: Kajima Institute Publishing Co., Ltd, 2001.

Kawabata, Yasunari. *The Old Capital,* trans. J. Martin Holman. Berkeley: Counterpoint Press, 2006.

Krausse, Joachim, and Claude Lichtenstein, eds. *Your Private Sky: R. Buckminster Fuller, The Art of Design Science.* Baden: Lars Müller Publishers, 1999.

Kronenburg, Robert. *Houses in Motion.* West Sussex: Wiley-Academy, 1995.

Leroi-Gourhan, André. *Gesture and Speech,* trans. Anna Bostock Berger. Cambridge, MA and London: The MIT Press, 1993.

Libeskind, Daniel. *Breaking Ground: An Immigrant's Journey from Poland to Ground Zero.* New York: Riverhead Books, 2004.

Libeskind, Daniel. *Daniel Libeskind: The Space of Encounter.* New York: Universe Publishing, 2000.

Lima, Manuel. *Visual Complexity: Mapping Patterns of Information.* New York: Princeton Architectural Press, 2011.

McCoy, Esther. *Case Study Houses 1945–1962.* Los Angeles: Hennessey & Ingalls, 1977.

Mack, Gerhard, and Herzog & de Meuron. *Herzog & de Meuron 1992–1996. Das Gesamtwerk, Band 3. The Complete Works, Volume 3,* ed. Gerhard Mack. Basel, Boston, Berlin: Birkhäuser, 2005.

Mahar-Keplinger, Lisa. *Grain Elevators.* New York: Princeton Architectural Press, 1993.

Meikle, Jeffery L. *American Plastic: A Cultural History.* New Brunswick: Rutgers University Press, 1995.

Meinig, D.W., ed. *The Interpretation of Ordinary Landscapes: Geographical Essays.* New York and Oxford: Oxford University Press, 1979.

Mihalyo, Daniel. *Wood Burners.* New York: Princeton Architectural Press, 1997.

MVRDV. *MVRDV: Km3: Excursions on Capacity.* Barcelona: Actar, 2005.

Nerdinger, Winfried, ed. *Frei Otto Complete Works: Lightweight Construction: Natural Design.* Basel, Boston, and Berlin: Birkhäuser, 2005.

Nørretranders, Tor. *The User Illusion: Cutting Consciousness Down to Size.* New York: Viking Penguin, 1998.

Otto, Frei, and Bodo Rasch. *Finding Form: Towards an Architecture of the Minimal.* Berlin: Edition Axel Menges, 1995.

Pallasmaa, Juhani. *The Thinking Hand.* West Sussex: John Wiley & Sons, Ltd., 2009.

Polanyi, Michael. *The Tacit Dimension.* Chicago and London: The University of Chicago Press, 1966.

Reed, Edward S. *Encountering the World: Toward an Ecological Psychology.* New York and Oxford: Oxford University Press, 1996.

Reiser, Jesse, and Nanako Umemoto, *Reiser+Umemoto.* West Sussex: John Wiley & Sons, Ltd., 1998.

Reiser, Jesse, and Nanako Umemoto. *Atlas of Novel Tectonics.* New York: Princeton Architectural Press, 2006.

Ronner, Heinz, and Sharad Jhaveri. *Louis I. Kahn: Complete Work 1935–1974.* Basel and Boston: Birkhäuser, 1987.

Rosenberg, Daniel, and Anthony Grafton. *Cartographies of Time: A History of the Timeline.* New York: Princeton Architectural Press, 2010.

Rudofsky, Bernard. *The Prodigious Builders: Notes Toward a Natural History of Architecture with Special Regard to Those Species that are Traditionally Neglected or Downright Ignored.* New York and London: Harcourt Brace Jovanovich, 1977.

Rudofsky, Bernard. *Architecture Without Architects: A Short Introduction to Non-Pedigreed Architecture.* Albuquerque: University of New Mexico Press, 1987.

Sadler, Simon. *Archigram: Architecture Without Architecture.* Cambridge, MA and London: The MIT Press, 2005.

Steele, James. *Eames House: Charles and Ray Eames.* London: Phaidon Press, 1994.

Tsukamoto, Yoshiharu. *WindowScape: Window Behaviourology.* Singapore: Page One, 2012.

Tufte, Edward R. *Visual Explanations.* Cheshire: Graphics Press LLC, 1997.

Tufte, Edward R. *Beautiful Evidence.* Cheshire: Graphics Press LLC, 2006.

Twombly, Robert. *Louis Kahn: Essential Texts.* New York and London: W.W. Norton & Co., 2003.

Tyng, Alexandra. *Beginnings: Louis I. Kahn's Photography of Architecture.* New York: Wiley & Sons, 1984.

Ursprung, Philip, ed. *Herzog & de Meuron: Natural History.* Baden: Lars Müller Publishers, 2002.

Venturi, Robert. *Complexity and Contradiction in Architecture.* New York: The Museum of Modern Art, 1966.

Venturi, Robert, Denise Scott Brown, and Steven Izenour. *Learning from Las Vegas: The Forgotten Symbolism of Architectural Form.* Cambridge, MA and London: The MIT Press, 1977.

Wenders, Wim. *The Logic of Images: Essays and Conversations,* trans. Michael Hofmann. London and Boston: Faber & Faber, 1992.

Wilde, Ann and Jürgen, eds. *Karl Blossfeldt: Fotografie.* Ostfilden: Cantz, 1994.

Wilde, Ann and Jürgen, eds. *Karl Blossfeldt: Working Collages,* trans. Christopher Jenkin-Jones. Cambridge, MA and London: The MIT Press, 2001.

Wurman, Richard Saul. *What Will Be Has Always Been: The Words of Louis I. Kahn.* New York: AccessPress, Ltd. and Rizzoli International Publications, Inc., 1986.

Image Credits

Figures 1.9 and 1.10	Courtesy Bill Rankin (Yale University), www.radicalcartography.net
Figures 1.11 and 1.12	Courtesy MVRDV
Figure 1.16	Courtesy Archigram Archives
Figures 1.22 and 1.23	Courtesy Atelier Bow-Wow
Figure 1.28	Minneapolis Institute of Arts, Gift of Elaine Dines Cox and Kris Cox, 98.265.10. © 2012 Karl Blossfeldt Archiv / Ann u. Jürgen Wilde, Köln/Artists Rights Society (ARS), NY
Figures 1.29 and 1.31	© 2012 Artists Rights Society (ARS), New York / VG Bild-Kunst, Bonn
Figure 2.6	© Architectural Archives of the University of Pennsylvania
Figure 3.5	© Studio Daniel Libeskind
Figures I1.1–I1.4	Courtesy Atelier Bow-Wow and Yoshiharu Tsukamoto
Figures 4.1 and 4.2	Digital Image © The Museum of Modern Art/Licensed by SCALA/Art Resource, NY. © Architectural Archives of the University of Pennsylvania
Figure 4.3	Courtesy Reiser + Umemoto
Figures 4.4 and 4.6	Courtesy Olson Kundig Architects
Figures 4.22–4.26	Courtesy Toyo Ito & Associates, Architects
Figure 5.8	Courtesy Eames Office © Vitra Design Museum
Figures 5.9–5.11	© 2012 Eames Office, LLC (eamesoffice.com)
Figure 6.3	Hirshhorn Museum and Sculpture Garden, Smithsonian Institution, Joseph H. Hirshhorn Bequest Fund, 1998
Figure 6.5	Courtesy Diller Scofidio + Renfro
Figures 7.7–7.9	Courtesy The Estate of R. Buckminster Fuller
Figures I2.1–I2.10	Courtesy Reiser + Umemoto

Index

Page numbers in *italics* indicate figures.